Counsel
Fit
For A
KING

Fanny Mayro
Christmas Eve 2012

Mike Baker

Counsel
Fit
For A
KING

Leadership Lessons from the
Old Testament Kings

HEARTSPRING PUBLISHING · JOPLIN, MISSOURI

A division of College Press Publishing Co.
Toll-free order line 800-289-3300
On the web at www.collegepress.com

Cover design by Mark A. Cole

Library of Congress Cataloging-in-Publication Data

Baker, Mike, 1965 Feb. 1–
    Counsel fit for a king: leadership lessons from the Old Testament
kings/ by Mike Baker.
        p. cm.
    ISBN 0-89900-922-0 (pbk.)
    1. Christian leadership—Biblical teaching.   2. Bible. O.T. Kings—
Criticism, interpretation, etc.   I. Title.
    BS680.L4B34 2003
    253—dc22

                                                        2003022625

For lack of guidance
a nation falls,
but many advisors
make a victory sure.

Proverbs 11:14

Plans fail
for lack of counsel,
but with many advisors
they succeed.

Proverbs 15:22

And in abundance of counselors
there is victory.

Proverbs 24:6b (NASB)

Table of Contents

Contents

Introduction

At the beginning of this book it is fair to ask if there is room for another book about leadership. What more could possibly be said concerning leadership? Virtually everywhere you look, there are numerous books written by different leaders from business, organizational, and church backgrounds. These books propose to give you ten, fifteen, or twenty (pick a number) principles for great leadership. And those of us who see ourselves as leaders buy them. We are hoping to learn from those who have proven track records in the area of leadership.

If you've read anything on leadership you will recognize some common encouragements. For example, many leadership books talk about the necessity of eliminating the people on your team who have limited abilities, gifts, or passions so you can get the job done. Most pastors would shout a

> "If we get the right people on the bus, the right people in the right seats and the wrong people off the bus, then we'll figure out how to take it someplace great."
>
> Jim Collins, *Good to Great* (New York: Harper Collins, 2001), p. 41.

hearty, "Amen!" We believe that good leadership begins with having the right people on our staff. We realize the need for gifted people, passionately focused on their ministries, but how many of us have the power to walk into a meeting and tell the board we're letting someone go because he isn't the right person for the job? Even if we did have that authority, how many of us could pull it off without causing a major controversy in the congregation?

Other leadership books insist that we should focus on a few things and forget everything else. That sounds great, but how

> "They know the most valuable asset leaders have is a powerful 'no' muscle. And they know that this muscle needs to be flexed every time an opportunity, no matter how noble the cause, threatens to lure them from the task God assigned to them."
>
> Bill Hybels, *Courageous Leadership* (Grand Rapids: Zondervan, 2002), p. 235.

many of us really feel like we can spend more time honing the sermon that will touch hundreds and ignore the "urgent" phone messages from the high needs person who must talk to us today? Many of us have job descriptions that are really several positions wrapped into one. The truth is, much of our time is taken up by the emergencies and crises of our flocks. We often spread ourselves so thin, we can't do anything well. It would be nice to fulfill our callings to focus primarily on the gifts we are most passionate about, but often real life ministry calls us to direct time and energy into the menial and less desirable but necessary pastoral tasks. Even though we agree with this leadership proposition, is it really ever practical?

The point is that many times after reading a leadership book we are loaded down with a new list of principles that just aren't practical. Most of the time, we walk away thinking, "What a great idea, but I could never do that where I am." Worse, we might mistakenly conclude that we must not have the gift of leadership, because we are so far from the model being proposed.

Hopefully, this book is different. It does not propose to give you a surefire formula for success as a leader. You should not walk away from this reading feeling inadequate in your leadership ability. Most leaders don't need more lists. What we need is constant exposure to other leaders in a variety of leadership situations. We need some real leadership examples that we can observe. We need people we can relate to who are in similar situations. Many of us don't need another "how to" book. We need a book of observation. And that's what this book is: a stroll through different leadership settings and situations. Hopefully, the notes we take along the way will help us formulate personal leadership lessons. The chapters which follow are not in order of importance or priority. Each leadership story stands on it's own. On the other hand, each is a part of a larger historical whole from which we can all learn. And where exactly can we find leadership examples?

This book proposes to find leadership wisdom in the leaders of the Old Testament. God's first group of "called out ones" was a people called the Israelites. They began their existence under the leadership of God's appointed leader, Moses, and then his successor, Joshua. After Joshua led the people into the Promised Land and divided up the inheritance among the tribes, he also died leaving the people of God with no real leadership structure. They floundered for years as judges periodically rallied the entire nation around a cause, but they were virtually without leadership.

For 300 years, from approximately 1400–1100 B.C., Israel had a total of thirteen judges who delivered them from their enemies and governed them.

Before I go any further, let me interject an important observation. God never wanted kings! He was the rightful King of His people. His design was for Israel to follow His leadership through obeying the laws and observing His feasts and festivals along with their respective sacrifices. When Samuel cried to God because the people were asking for a king, God told him, "It is not you they have rejected, but they have rejected me as their king." (1 Sam 8:7). This system of leadership was not God's original design, but He used a series of kings to accomplish His will. This is the eternal omniscience of God at work. Woven throughout the lives of these kings is the consistent thread of His eternal will and purpose. Throughout this writing we will try to note the more obvious threads. But every story that follows should be taken in the context of God's desire to be King of his people and his ability to accomplish that through leaders both good and bad.

After the people cried out for a king like the rest of the nations around them, God gave them what they wanted. The beginning was relatively successful with the lengthy reigns of three kings, but soon the kingdom was divided up into the two kingdoms of Judah and Israel. All told, there was a period of about 450 years during which the leaders of God's people were kings. It is an examination of these kings and their lives that will guide us in our study because in them we find leaders like us.

For starters, most of the kings came to the throne with absolutely zero king experience. Not only did King Saul lack experience, he had no example to follow. He took control of a loosely organized kingdom of tribes that were scattered from Dan to

Beersheba. Since the occupation of the Land of Canaan, they had been led by warrior judges, spiritual priests, and dedicated prophets. Up until that point, the people of God were alternately punished for their unfaithfulness and delivered in times of repentance. They were sometimes protected by His mighty acts and at others handed over to surrounding nations by His providence. The people of God experienced great victories only as they rallied behind the boldness of men and women of faith. But now, they had a king. How would Saul inspire, protect, motivate, and lead this diverse group of people?

Certainly, there would need to be significant management-level changes made in order for Saul to lead effectively. Who could he trust? He would need authority, but how much? Simply put, Saul didn't know how to be king. All he knew was that in the course of one day, Samuel anointed him to be the first king of Israel, placing the burden of leadership directly on him. Perhaps that's why on inauguration day we find Saul hiding among the luggage! The prospect of leadership overwhelmed him, because he lacked experience.

As I read through the books of Samuel and Kings, I also noticed that many of the succeeding kings came to the throne lacking experience. Most of them inherited the throne when their father king died. Many of them took the throne by brute force, motivated by their lust for power. Some of them were simply the last living relative of a family. Some were appointed by popular opinion. But few had prior experience before coming to this powerful leadership position.

> Baasha became Israel's king by assassinating Nadab around 910 B.C. Twenty-four years later, his son Elah was assassinated by Zimri. (See 1 Kings 15:28 & 16:10.)

There was no Jerusalem Seminary where they could major in King Theory. There were no books entitled, "Nineteen Principles for Being the King of God's People." They couldn't go to Gath or Egypt for a hands-on, king internship program. They simply found themselves in charge, and from a leadership standpoint only a few of them found success.

Many of today's young church leaders find themselves in the same predicament. While few inherit a ministry from their father and none, that I know of, murdered someone to get their position, most feel a calling to be a leader in the Church. For some, this is simply a logical decision. An individual knows he/she is a leader and decides to use that gift in vocational ministry. For others, it is a very spiritual experience. During a prayer time or moment of devotion, they realize the Holy Spirit is moving them to surrender to God's plans of leadership in their lives. Whatever the motivating factor however, most come into a position of leadership without a real knowledge of how to lead people. There is a moment in every church leader's life when he leans back in his office chair, glances at his stack of freshly printed business cards, marvels at the fact he has his own extension, and stares at a sparse collection of ministry related books on the shelf. At this moment, he thinks almost audibly to himself, "Wow, I'm in ministry." Then it hits him; "What do I do now?"

Of course, many have earned degrees at Bible college. Most have completed internship programs designed to give them field experience. A small percentage even read all those books assigned in school. But few are truly prepared for the diverse makeup of people they will encounter in the church. Most church leaders come to their position of leadership with no real experience and no concrete plan for leading. Like Saul, they wonder how they will inspire, protect, motivate, and lead such a diverse bunch of people, especially when they're not sure who they are as leaders.

A study of the kings of the Old Testament will also reveal that many of them were very young when they came into their leadership roles. David was the youngest of his brothers, a mere shepherd boy, when Samuel anointed him as king. More than likely, he was a teen-ager, but that's nothing compared to two other kings. Joash was seven years old when he came to the

> Ironically, these three kings were arguably three of the best kings to ever sit on the throne and govern God's people. Each enjoyed a reign of over 30 years and worked hard to prevent idolatry from leading the people astray.

throne of Judah and Josiah was eight when he took the throne (I wonder if they had to ask for booster seats). Not only did most of the kings of Israel not have courtly experience, most lacked life experience early in their reigns. Yet these boys were the bosses of men who had defeated armies and accomplished great heroics in battle. They were asked to set the religious tone for a nation of millions. Their judgments and decisions became law that those around them followed with great allegiance. Luckily, they were too young to know how impossible it was for a kid to be king. There is no way they could live up to the leadership challenges they faced. Based on their lack of life experience, they were surely some of the most unqualified leaders in the history of the world.

Today's church leaders find themselves with a similar challenge. The seminary grad often comes to his first ministry younger than the elders, less experienced than the married couples with children, and more naïve than the business people in the congregation. But he has the title of leader. Many inherit oversight of a large budget when they can barely balance their personal checkbook. Part of the job includes marriage counseling for troubled couples, while they are themselves struggling to juggle marriage and ministry. Church leaders are called to set the spiritual tone for the group they are leading at the same time they are in the process of discovering what Christ is creating in them. Like these kid kings, they are called upon to nurture the congregation spiritually, make decisions with the wisdom of an elder, and have enough experience to cast vision and raise the funds to pay for it. They find themselves with a title of leadership, but they have little life experience to help them accomplish the task. And when is someone experienced? The truth is, most of us will spend all of our ministry years trying to experience enough of life's circumstances to earn the wisdom and the respect that comes with it. There is no substitute for the sheer amount of time this process takes.

We find our leadership selves in the lives of these kings because we come into similar situations. Because of their unfaithfulness to God, the kingdoms of Israel and Judah were in constant turmoil. With few exceptions, they were threatened, invaded, conquered, killed, and taxed by various enemies on every side. The land "flowing with milk and honey" never really became the promised land that God intended because His people didn't trust Him enough to lead them. Their religious system, complete with rules, rituals, and festivals, had become empty for many and at times virtually nonexistent. During much of this royal history, because of economic hardship and foreign turmoil, the people had

> The Passover was not fully celebrated for a period of about 500 years from the time of the judges to the reign of King Josiah. (See 1 Kings 23:22.)

divided loyalties. In short, the kings of Israel became leaders in the harshest of conditions. They sat on the throne of kingdoms that were at times financially unstable, spiritually dead, physically exhausted, and personally discouraged.

There is no doubt that God's church is His way of accomplishing His will in the world today, but a quick glance and you will see a strong resemblance between the people of Israel and the people who attend First Church of Your Hometown, USA. Many leaders come into a congregation with the zeal to change the world and find a group of people who lifelessly limp through Sunday after Sunday, playing church. Many ministers have incredible ideas to reach out and become Christ in the community, but monetary resources just aren't available to make them happen. Other church leaders find it impossible to motivate people who are just worn out by life. And worst of all, many of them are forced to spend their time settling silly disputes between Christians who should know better. These situations make it difficult for the most experienced of leaders, how much more the novice?

Many of us have read leadership books and thought, "I could be a great leader if I had a budget like the author probably has." Or "That guy wouldn't last five minutes with my board." Or, "I wish someone could see the way these people act." The truth is that most churches pose one or more of the challenges mentioned above. It doesn't take long for a pastor to realize a church is not a workplace utopia. While we catch glimpses of God's work among us from time to time, we honestly spend many days wondering if we are making any difference at all. It's hard to lead a kingdom, and it's hard to lead a church, but maybe if we look behind the scenes of these kings' lives, we can learn something to guide us in our own.

That's the journey we are embarking on together. I came to the kings of the Old Testament with an open mind. I tried not to impose any leadership ideas or terms on the stories. I literally sat down with a pen, some paper and a Bible and started to read. When something happened to a king that resembled something a church leader might experience, I wrote it down. Some were "how to's" and many were "how not to's," but when it was all said and done, I felt there was something to be learned. Many of these kings were inexperienced at leadership and at life, and the organization they were responsible for was often falling apart. But in the midst of this, I found God working. The leaders in the books of Samuel, Kings, and Chronicles are not an honor roll of leadership, but they led the people of God, and somehow He used them. Most of them could have done better, none of them were perfect, but all of them were leaders of God's people. And, by the grace of God, so are we.

If you're still reading, it's probably because you sense a leadership call deep inside and you have a desire to grow in your leadership. In the following pages we will examine real life leaders in their greatest victories and worst defeats. We will find great faith and greater unfaithfulness. We will find good decisions and terrible judgments. We will find leaders who don't know what they're doing, and a God who always has a plan. And somewhere in between, we might find our leadership selves.

CHAPTER ONE

Humility

"But am I not a Benjamite, from the *smallest* tribe of Israel, and is not my clan the *least* of all the clans of the tribe of Benjamin? Why do you say such things to me?" (1 Samuel 9:21).

"Do you think it is a small matter to become the king's son-in-law? I'm only a poor man and little known" (1 Samuel 18:23).

"For rebellion is like the sin of divination, and arrogance like the evil of idolatry" (1 Samuel 15:23).

The best place to begin is, well, the beginning, and that's exactly what Saul represents when it comes to the line of earthly kings in the history of God's people. The Israelites had cried out for a king and though God warned them through the prophet Samuel that it may be more than they bargained for, he chose the son of Kish to be king. And where did He find him? Looking for donkeys.

> "One manifestation of a humble attitude is the willingness to lay bare one's afflictions, vulnerabilities, and insecurities—a willingness to share with others that one has the same human frailties that they have."
>
> Michael A. Zigarelli, *Management by Proverbs* (Chicago: Moody Press, 1999), p. 60.

These were the humble beginnings for the man who would become Israel's first king. We can picture him wandering through the hill country of Ephraim saying, "Here donkey, donkey." Kish had some missing animals, so he sent Saul along with a servant to find them. After a few days of unsuccessful searching, Saul wanted to return home for fear that his dad would forget the donkeys and begin to worry about his son, but the servant insisted that the prophet Samuel might be the perfect DPS (donkey positioning system). Since the prophet was in town, Saul agreed and they found the man of God. Can you imagine the conversation? "Oh, great prophet of God, do you know where our donkeys are?" But Samuel didn't want to talk about the missing donkeys. "The donkeys have been found," he assured the searching son, "but while you're concerned about donkeys, all of Israel is searching for you."

What a strange thing to say. Saul was taller than most, but he didn't consider himself someone that the whole nation would be concerned about. His family wasn't exceptionally large or power-

Saul's tribe, Benjamin, was almost totally destroyed by the rest of Israel in response to their offense at Gibeah. The Israelite army eliminated all but 600 Benjamite men. (See Judges 20:46-48.)

ful. Why would the prophet make a fuss over him? Yet at supper, the special treatment continued. The prophet gave Saul his personal portion of the lamb and a place of honor at the head of the table. Then Samuel anointed Saul and sent him on a scavenger hunt of sorts to dis-

cover the spirit of leadership God was pouring out on him. On this journey he would meet two men with news from home about the donkeys. Next, he would then encounter three men going up to Bethel who would give him loaves of bread, and finally he would join a prophetic parade in Gibeah. It was here that the Spirit of the Lord would change him as Saul prophesied with the others. The incredible events of this trip forever changed Saul's life, but he still didn't assume that he could be king.

When he returned home, his uncle asked him where he had been and if he knew how worried the whole family was. Saul simply told his uncle that the prophet Samuel had told them about the donkey's return, but his humility kept him from saying anything further. There was no bragging about getting to go first in the prophet's buffet line. He didn't mention that he had been anointed king. The gift of prophecy and the change of heart all remained a secret, that is until Samuel called all the people to the Lord at Mizpah to announce God's choice for king.

Mizpah literally means "a watch tower."

To the family's great surprise, Samuel was indicating God's call on their relative—Saul, son of Kish. But when the trumpets blew and the people cheered, Saul was nowhere to be found. I suppose the prophet could have given the standard awards-ceremony response, "Accepting the kingship on behalf of Saul this evening. . . ." But instead, he inquired whether Saul had come to the holy gathering, and when his family said he had, the search was on. Finally, after a few embarrassing moments, they found Saul hiding among the Samsonite (no relation to the former judge with long hair). At this point in the journey, Saul seemed to display a humility that God must have seen. As he bashfully made his way to the front of the crowd, they noticed his incredible physique and height. God had given them a king! "Long live King Saul!"

God's second choice for king was called in a similar way. When Samuel came to Jesse's house in Bethlehem and announced that one of Jesse's sons would be anointed the next king of God's people, the old prophet and proud father naturally assumed it would be the oldest son. But that wasn't God's plan. Some of the other brothers were strong and some were handsome, but God had chosen none of them. When Samuel inquired as to whether there was yet another son, Jesse indicated that indeed his youngest was out in the field watching sheep. But surely, this lowly shepherd was not the great leader God was calling to the throne!

> The biblical account of Samuel's visit to Bethlehem lists the first three sons of Jesse as Eliab, Abinadab, and Shammah. In all, seven of David's brothers passed before the prophet before David was called. (See 1 Samuel 16:6-10.)

David was summoned from the field hearing that the holy man was calling his name. His hair was wild and his face was boyish and innocent. He came to his father and humbly asked what was needed. Immediately, the prophet knew that this was the one God had called, and he anointed him king. God told Samuel that man looks on the outside, but He looks at the heart. It must have been a humble spirit that the Almighty saw. David's humility didn't end there. After he killed the giant, he continued to fulfill his duty as the king's personal harpist (a job way beneath any warrior!).

> "My heart is not proud, O LORD, my eyes are not haughty; I do not concern myself with great matters or things too wonderful for me" (Psalm 131:1).

Later, after he had proven himself in many battles and victories, he declined the king's offer to become his son-in-law thinking it to be above his worth and standing. He was a humble man.

I don't think it coincidental that God's first two choices for king had very humble beginnings. Neither of them believed for an instant that they deserved the throne, and neither thought they were capable. Theirs was not the kind of feigned humility that secretly desires the accolades of men while claiming to be in it for the kingdom. We're talking about a sincere belief of unworthiness for a position of honor. Brennan Manning, in his book *Ruthless Trust* describes these two best: "Humble men and women do not have a low opinion of themselves; they have no opinion of themselves, because they so rarely think about themselves." When Samuel came to both Saul and David to anoint them as king, they weren't putting on a show; they had no opinion of themselves as king. They were sincerely surprised, shocked, incredulous, and maybe even a little scared. They must have felt unworthy both in ability and social position. Church leaders may note something here.

God's call on the leader's life today is no less puzzling than His choices for king. Why would He choose sinful people to lead His Body? Why would He allow a message of forgiveness to be spoken from lips that need repentance? Why would God call men and women who cannot grasp who God is to lead others to Him? God uses unworthy people to accomplish His purpose through the church. This means that every Christian leader today should begin with the same attitude as Saul and David. The first question of a godly leader is, "Who am I that I should lead?" These two kings didn't think, "I'd be a lousy king." They never thought about being king at all. The idea that they would sit on the throne never entered their minds.

Great leadership in the church begins with those who have this attitude. Whether you are pastoring a congregation of twenty, are a youth minister with forty students, or a music pastor with a hundred voice choir, you should be humbly amazed to think that God would be able to use even you. When a congregation says, "Come and lead us"; when an organization asks someone to join with them; when people look to the leader for spiritual advice; the reply should be a humble, "Who am I?" It should come as no surprise that Jesus set this example in an eternal way. "Who, being in very nature

> "It's not that God has a problem with seeing His children in places of honor and glory. In truth He longs to exalt them. What concerns Him is the upward mobility as defined by the world."
> Bill Hybels, *Descending into Greatness* (Grand Rapids: Zondervan, 1993), p. 20.

God, did not consider equality with God something to be grasped" (Philippians 2:6).

In the days of Samuel, when God's eyes roamed the earth searching the hearts of Israel for just the right king, He spotted two guys who were humble. What an awesome day it was when the oil of God ran down the face of each of these leaders. It was a day each would never forget—a day when the lowly were exalted, a day when the last became first, a day when the weak became strong. On that day, these men went from lowly, obscure herdsman to men who would sit on the throne. God still seeks men and women of humble spirit who will lead His people. He desires to put them in positions of leadership and influence. And He knows that great leadership begins with an attitude of humility and those are the people He often calls.

How do we as modern-day, godly leaders display this kind of humility? I believe it begins with attitude, moves into action, and is finally lived out as an example to others.

First, humility begins with an attitude of contentment. Saul and David were apparently content with being shepherds for life. This is not the kind of contentment that becomes apathetic, but the kind that has to do with trust in God and fulfillment in each moment of ministry. Many Christian leaders are always looking for the next thing. There is a quest in our culture for bigger and better. To move up the ladder of success. Church leaders are not immune to this pull. Some pastors want larger congregations. Some want to do ministry in better geographical locations. Still others want a title that will bring them some sort of prestige or notoriety. These desires are not what being a leader for God is all about. You see, humility begins in the heart with an attitude of contentment—with who you are, where you are, and what you're called to do.

> ". . . for I have learned to be content whatever the circumstances" (Phil 4:11).

David was content to shepherd a flock in Bethlehem and write songs on his harp. Saul had no aspirations for greatness. He was content serving his household by looking for the stray donkeys. He didn't complain. At his father's bidding he went, and every indication is that he did not think the task to be beneath him. If you want to be a great leader, you need to ask yourself a question that cuts to the heart of the matter. If you find yourself serving in God's kingdom in relative obscurity, never receiving any recognition for the great things you accomplish, yet touching lives for Jesus, will you be okay with that? The answer to that question will reveal to yourself and to God whether or not you have an attitude of humility.

Truthfully, most of us struggle with nonrecognition. It feels good when people notice. Unfortunately, the obscure places are

> "Better is one day in your courts than a thousand elsewhere. I would rather be a doorkeeper in the house of my God . . . " (Psalm 84:10).

where God sometimes forges the hearts of His greatest leaders. He knows if He has our hearts in the small places, He will have them in the powerful places. God wants leaders who are content with who they are, where they are, and what they are.

This contentment in turn becomes action as we learn to walk by faith in a different way. You see, only those who are content with the grace that God has given them will be able to completely yield to His leading. Faith, by it's very nature can be a full-speed-ahead sprint into the darkness at God's bidding. And humility is a requirement for running this way. Saul and David were able to become the leaders God desired because they knew they alone weren't capable of the task, so they had to trust in God. This is where Saul eventually stumbled.

In 1 Samuel 15 we find the story of Saul's arrogance. The Lord had sent him on a mission to destroy the Amalekites. God was specific. Kill the king and the animals; everything that lives. But as God gave Saul the victory, he decided that he would keep some of the sheep and that he would spare Agag, the king.

> "Agag may be the title of the kings of Amalek, like Pharaoh of Egypt."
>
> F.N. and M.A. Peloubet, eds., *Smith's Bible Dictionary* (Nashville: Thomas Nelson, 1962), p. 22.

This is when God tells Samuel that He regretted making Saul the king. A man who had once shown a tendency towards humility, had now become his own authority in deciding not to carry out God's entire plan. God grieved, Samuel cried, and the throne was taken from Saul. Why? Saul no longer followed God by faith, because his heart told him to trust himself. His lack of humility had caused him not to run in faith-sight allegiance to God.

This is where God's leaders often get sidetracked. Adultery, arrogance, tyranny, laziness, and materialism too often creep into the leader's life. It often devastates the flock and hurts the reputation of God, but it should come as no surprise. The reason God's leaders so often find themselves morally bankrupt is that they have forgotten their humble beginnings. Samuel says in verse 23 of chapter 15, "arrogance is like the evil of idolatry." Once God's leader thinks he is self-sufficient, he will no longer follow God by faith. And if you can't lead with trusting allegiance to God and His leadership, then you can't be a faithful leader for Him.

When we learn to follow God by faith because of a humble understanding of who we are, we are able to model humility to those around us. I believe others are nurtured when we as leaders don't have all the answers, but we keep going in our calling despite the uncertainty. After all,

> "Now faith is being sure of what we hope for and certain of what we do not see" (Hebrews 11:1).

one certainty in the Christian walk is that it is uncertain. We don't know how things will work out, or exactly when God is going to move. Because He has proven Himself to us in the past, we simply walk on, trusting that He will! When those around us see that we humbly trust even when we don't fully understand, they are encouraged in their faith as well.

David displayed humility before his mighty men after he had been anointed king, but was on the run from jealous King Saul. God had promised him through Samuel that someday he would sit on the throne, but how would it work and when would it happen?

> "You have treated me well, but I have treated you badly. You have just now told me of the good you did to me; the LORD delivered me into your hands, but you did not kill me" (1 Samuel 24:17-18).

David didn't know, but he was careful not to run ahead of God. On two separate occasions, David had the opportunity to kill the only man between him and the throne and did not. Why? Humility. David knew that God was in control, so he led by faith and humbly waited on God's timing. I'm sure his men wanted to kill Saul. Without a doubt many of them thought, "He should have killed him when he had the chance." I'm sure many became impatient waiting for the transfer of power, but David would only refer to his enemy as the

"LORD's anointed." He modeled to others humble faith by his example.

The body of Christ is in need of servant leaders who are not driven by the success mentality that has become prevalent in the American church. People may follow the arrogant for a time, but in the end these leaders will be shown for what they really are. Revolutions may begin with spoiled dictators, but they don't last forever. True movements of God begin when down-to-earth men and women of God who consider themselves nothing follow God no matter the cost. David and Saul both began with this trait, and that's why God chose them to lead. Today's leaders are no different. God will raise up those who have humbled themselves under His grace and are content simply to be in His service.

CHAPTER TWO

The Word Is Found

"I have found the Book of the Law in the temple of the LORD"
(2 Kings 22:8).

"When the king heard the words of the Book of the Law, he tore
his robes" (2 Kings 22:11).

"He read in their hearing all the words of the Book of the
Covenant, which had been found in the temple of the LORD"
(2 Kings 23:2).

It was not uncommon during my years of ministry at
Kissimmee, Florida, to come face to face on a Sunday morning with twenty unprepared, bored, and tired high school
students. You guessed it—Sunday
school class. I could hardly blame
them for being bored and tired.
Honestly, most Sundays I felt the
same. In between setting up for
the days' activities and children's
church, I was supposed to stir
these less than fertile hearts with
something that would interest
them and change their souls at the
same time.

> "Only God's truth can accurately and
> authoritatively reject false values and
> distinguish that which is true. An
> addiction to God's truth will change
> our minds, our lives and our culture."
> Joseph Stowell, *The Dawn's Early Light* (Chicago: Moody Press, 1990), p. 57.

From time to time, in the middle of my talk, I would ask
them to look up a verse in the Bible. Usually, I could only count
on a couple of them having a Bible with them, but one young man
had a system. When it came time for the Bible verses, he reached
under the same couch in the same spot and pulled out his Bible.
He'd simply dust it off and turn to the verse we were looking at.
I asked him why he left his Bible under the couch. "It's the only

time of the week I use it, so I keep it here for when I need it," he replied. At least he was honest!

Unfortunately, I could see a parallel between the use of the Word in my teaching and his use of the Word on a daily basis. I taught from a solid Bible perspective. My teachings were orthodox. I used Scripture enough to give it a guest appearance or when I really needed it to make a point, but it wasn't the focus of our time together. In my quest for relevance and the desire to be interesting, I had buried the Book.

Many of today's church leaders have buried the Word. We have put it in a safe place where we can get it if needed, but too much of the time, we lead on our spiritual instinct alone. Of course, this is as absurd as a Bible sitting under the couch only to be used once a week during Sunday school class. God's leader cannot lead God's people well without giving God's Word a place of prominence. The people of God are in desperate need for direction from today's leader, and that leadership will come from the Word not from cleverness of speech or intellect. Today's leader

> "My message and my preaching were not with wise and persuasive words, but with a demonstration of the Spirit's power" (1 Corinthians 2:4).

may spend an incredible amount of time fashioning the perfect speech, but only the eternal truth of God's Word will make our words relevant. As a matter of fact, they'll become more than relevant, they'll become vital. Only the truth of God's Word has this kind of power. It's time to pull the Word out from under the spiritual couch and give it rightful priority again. God's leader for today would do well to learn from a young king who found the Word again.

Josiah wanted to make repairs to the temple. Over the years, it had fallen from its original splendor and Josiah had a vision for bringing the glory back. This was a sizable project for any king to tackle, but even more remarkable because this king was only twenty-six years old and had inherited a wicked, idolatrous people from his pagan father and grandfather. Perhaps the prophet Jeremiah got to Josiah early (by this time

> The temple built by Solomon retained its original glory for only a short time. Five years after Solomon's death, Shishak the king of Egypt attacked Jerusalem and plundered the temple. (See 1 Kings 14:25.)

he had been king for 18 years—he was eight when he started), and that's why he ended up following God whole-heartedly. Whatever the reason, we know that from an early age this king was trying to lead people back to God after years of rebellion, and that he

> Jeremiah began his prophetic ministry early in Josiah's reign (circa 627 BC) and continued to speak for God until Jerusalem was burned in 586.

accidentally managed to find *the Source* for godly leadership.

The story of this young reformer is found in both 2 Kings 22 and 2 Chronicles 34. He is toward the end of a frustrating string of mostly unfaithful kings. But Josiah was different from his predecessors. Apparently, purifying the land from all its wickedness was his political platform. After eighteen years of removing idols and shrines, he turned his attention to the temple. It had once been the glorious temple where God's glory dwelt among His people. It was an extravagant building constructed by his rich ancestor Solomon, but years of apathy and disrespect had left it in disrepair. The gold didn't glisten, the doors creaked from neglect, and the tapestries were worn and colorless.

Josiah instructed his officers to begin a campaign of raising money from the people who came to worship at the temple. The priests who ministered at the temple's entrances apparently spent some time collecting offerings from the Israelites until they had enough to pay for materials and labor. Finally, in the twenty-sixth year of his life, Josiah was ready to complete the project he had dreamed about. He instructed his palace secretary, Shaphan, to go to Hilkiah the High Priest to get the money and go to the Jerusalem Home Depot. He was instructed to buy the materials and pay the laborers. Let the work begin. In the process, Hilkiah found something that would help rebuild more than just a building.

In preparation for remodeling, Hilkiah had begun some cleaning of the temple area. Josiah's grandfather, Manasseh, had thoroughly desecrated this holy home. He had actually allowed some idols in the temple, some storage areas that contained false gods, a sewing room for those making priest clothes for Asherah, and rooms for male shrine prostitutes. In the process, the holy articles of the Lord had been shelved.

> Ironically, Manasseh means "forgetting," and this king of Judah forgot God. He led God's people in idolatry during much of his 55-year reign.

These once-sacred items had been stored away because they were made of gold and therefore valuable, but were no longer used by the people in proper worship of God.

It's possible that Hilkiah and his assistants were rummaging through some old idols, lamps, and incense bowls when they discovered a scroll. From the layers of dust, it was apparent it hadn't been read in a long time. Curiosity caused an assistant to unroll the sacred writings. He began to read the Book of the Law that the great leader Moses had copied for the people. Hilkiah must have shuddered to hear the Word of the Lord audibly for perhaps the first time. He obviously had happened upon something special. He immediately rolled up the scroll and waited for the right time to share his find.

Follow God's Thread

Finding the Book of the Covenant was undoubtedly God's design. Though His people had been unfaithful for years, He remained faithful. He revealed Himself yet again through the scrolls delivered to a godly king.

Not long after that, the secretary came in wearing a hard hat and giving orders for construction to begin. After some small talk about masons, mortar, and timbers, Hilkiah told Shaphan the good news. "I found the Book of the Law, the very words of God that I've heard about, tucked away in some storage closet. I wonder if the king has ever seen this?" Shaphan returned to the palace with doubly good news—the temple work had begun and the Word of God had been found! As the king's assistant began to read this message from God for His people, the king leapt from his throne, tore his royal robes, and fell face down on the ground. For years, the leaders of God had attempted to lead while ignoring the Word, and now Josiah had found it. This find forever changed his leadership. He spent the last thirteen years of his life learning, following, teaching, obeying, and leading by the Word of God. Could it be that today's leader could rejuvenate his leadership by pulling the Word from under the couch and following the example of this king?

In both of the scriptural accounts of this story, we find the words "Book of the Law" and "Book of the Covenant" used interchangeably to describe the words of life and truth that God had spoken to Moses in the mountain. It was the Jewish Bible. It was the way that God wanted these people to live. These words contained God's design for social harmony. But they were more than just rules (as the phrase "Book of the Law" may imply). These words were more than just laws, they were covenant words. They described an agreement that Almighty God had entered into with all who were descended from Abraham. This is the point. The Word of God shouldn't be hidden by the leaders because it represents a covenant of

> "In its time, of course, no one conceived of the Old Testament as one book. Each book had its own scroll, and a long book like Jeremiah would occupy a scroll twenty or thirty feet long. A Jewish person entering a synagogue would see stacks of scrolls, not a single book . . . ."
>
> Philip Yancey, *The Bible Jesus Read* (Grand Rapids: Zondervan, 1999), p. 21.

eternal proportions. To lose the Word is to lose the deal. To ignore the Word is to break the contract. To forget the Book of the Covenant is to miss a chance at relationship with God!

Nevertheless, since the days of David most of the kings had followed their own ways and forgotten these words. The results were devastating. Where God's Word is ignored chaos will follow.

This is the part of the story that is remarkable. The Word was right there under the people's noses—hidden in the temple all the time. It hadn't changed. The promises and warnings and condemnations still applied. It's just that the words had been forgotten, lost, forsaken. And it began gradually, with a king deciding that he didn't need the antiquated words of Scripture to lead his contemporary and socially advanced people.

Well, Josiah changed all that. He repented and led God's people for the remainder of his life by the authority of the Book. He led Israel to celebrate the Passover again (first time in hundreds of years). Josiah read the entire law in front of all the leaders and had them recommit to its teachings and laws. This young leader virtually eradicated idol worship from the land. He had begun down the right path as a leader in his youth, but he became a great leader when he found the Book. Its power and its words changed his reign.

If you desire to be a better leader for God, you may need to rediscover the Word of God. Of course, today the covenant of God is more than rules and regulations. The new Covenant was established by the living Word, whose life and teachings were preserved in a written word of grace called good news. If Josiah had reason to lead by the Word, the leader in today's church has even more. Not that God's desire for fellowship with His people is any different, but a bigger price has been paid. If you want the people who follow you to grow, take the advice of Richard Less.

> We've become so indoctrinated with the philosophy of church growth in this nation that we've forgotten what God says, and that's 'preach My Word' and then your church will grow ("Current Thoughts and Trends," December 2002).

But why? It's one thing to make claims about God's Word creating a better leader and a growing church, but what makes that so? Consider the following implications for leadership.

Leadership based on the Word of God brings personal and corporate conviction.

Did you notice the first thing that happened when Josiah heard the words of the Book read in his presence? He tore his robes. He probably fell prostrate on the floor and humbled himself as a sinner before God. The Word of God brings conviction into the life of the leader. There are times when leaders read the Bible for teaching purposes. There are other times when they study out of duty. But sometimes, in moments least expected, the Word of God hits them between the eyes, causes a convicting rip in their hearts, and makes

"Rend your heart and not your garments" (Joel 2:13).

them fall before God in awe of who He is and recognition of who they aren't. Godly leaders need this conviction. It grounds them and keeps them from becoming conceited. God's word continually reminds us of who we are—sinners who are saved by the grace of God. If we ignore the Word, we may be inclined to forget this simple truth—and so might our people.

The people of God also need a regular spiritual menu of biblical preaching and teaching from those who would lead for God. We may assume that Josiah and his people read the Book of the Law more than once after this dis-

"For the word of God is living and active. Sharper than any double-edged sword, it penetrates even to dividing soul and spirit, joints and marrow; it judges the thoughts and attitudes of the heart" (Hebrews 4:12).

covery. He realized as we should that only the Word of God has the power to cut to the heart of the matter and show people the error of their ways. This understanding breaks through the barriers and pretenses to who we actually are. It exposes our weaknesses and demonstrates our foolishness. In a word, the Scripture brings conviction to the people we are called to lead. I believe this is why there are several occasions in the Old Testament when the leader read the Book of the Law in its entirety in the audience of all the people. If our people are convicted by the Word and realize that we are as well, it is easier for them to follow us as a fellow traveler on a journey to God. But leadership enhanced by the Word goes beyond its ability to convict.

> Before his death, Moses commanded the elders of Israel to read the entire law to all of the people every seven years during the Feast of Tabernacles. (See Deuteronomy 31:9-13.)

Leadership based on the Word of God gives us a leadership standard.

Part of leading is being able to point people in the right direction. It won't take long for most leaders to realize their title is not the only reason people follow them. People follow in the long run because they think the leader has answers. And we're not talking about easy answers. The questions that today's church leader faces cannot be solved in one Sunday school lesson. These are questions of the soul—puzzles that have taken a lifetime to scramble. Complications that are beyond comprehension. How can the leader be expected to lead in the right direction? The Word of God gives the perfect standard.

The usher's room in our congregation is the nerve center for all of what our ushers do each week. In this room is a huge master seating chart of our auditorium. The ushers use this as a standard to know where the handicapped seats are, how many seats are in each section, and what seat numbers are where. If someone has a question about seating, our ushers have the perfect standard for helping. They simply refer to the chart on the wall. Some have used the chart so much and seen it so many times, they can answer the questions without looking at the chart. They are that familiar with the standard.

The answers to the questions are in the Word. Only in our continual guidance by the Book will we find answers for our people's lives. And only in our continual use of the Word will we prepare ourselves for years of leadership ahead. We will never get rid of the chart, but constant use will make us ready to help and lead by its truth. The kings of Israel led God's people astray because they neglected the words of the Book and chose to rely on their own "wisdom." Still today, many leaders attempt to lead based on their wisdom and of course fail just as miserably. We need to recommit to the standard of the Word of God in our leadership.

Leadership based on the Word of God gives authority.

There is no leadership without authority. For someone to effectively direct another, he must have some sort of authority over the one he is to lead. That authority may be because of a title the person holds (you have to follow your boss), the proven results of the leader's life, or just a belief that the leader is wise enough to lead. But none of these are sufficient when it comes to leading in the church. What today's leader needs is an authority that is higher than all of these. The Word gives church leaders this type of authority.

Arrogance aside, have you noticed that sometimes as church leaders we find ourselves timidly leading? Why is this? Because too many times we lead by ideas and innovations born of our minds and the input of our people. When these ideas are questioned (and they often are), the leader shrinks into timidity and waivers back and forth. It would seem that Jesus' brother knew this would happen to the people of God. That's why he encouraged his readers not to waiver in their faith (James 1:6). There is one way to keep us from wavering. We can confidently lead with courage when we have a firm foundation that we believe in with all of our heart. The Word of God is that for today's leader.

When we lead by the Word of God, there is less wavering because we know His Word is true. When our values, ideas, plans, and leadership are based on the Word of God, we have an authority like no other. This is why the prophets stood in front of king after faithless king and proclaimed words boldly. Many of them knew going in that they would be rejected, but the Lord had spoken, and their authority

> Ezekiel was forewarned that He was being sent to an "obstinate and stubborn" people. This, however, would not release him from speaking God's word with authority. He was told to speak whether they listened or not. (See Ezekiel 2:4-5.)

came from God. The great leader will derive his authority from God's Word and God's Word alone. When criticism comes (and it will), he can stand firm because his authority is from God. People are intrigued by that kind of leadership. All of these points are valuable to the leader of God, but the Word must be a part of today's church leadership because of what the Word stands for.

Leadership based on the Word of God is leadership of the covenant.

Why did God speak a word at all? Why did He begin with, "Let there be light" in Genesis 1? Why did He walk with Adam and Eve in the garden? Why did the Almighty tell Noah to build a boat in the desert? Why would the Eternal tell Abraham to count the stars? Why would The Perfect One choose to call sinful David a man after His own heart? Why? Because God has, from the beginning of time desired covenant with people.

This, it seems to me, is the crux of why we should lead. Leaders have discovered this relationship. We have entered into covenant with God. Through the blood of God's Son, we have become sons and daughters of God. He has become our Father. And that's why we lead. We desire to bring others into this same relationship. The whole point of leading people in the church is to connect them with a God who has spoken a covenant of peace with them and sealed it with His own blood. The only message we have for this world is the new covenant that is found in the Word of God, both living and written. Our leadership must be directed by the Word, for in it is the deal of a lifetime for all mankind— indeed, the deal of eternity—life with God in heaven. Josiah knew that the words of this newly discovered covenant book meant life to the people.

Josiah stood out among the kings as one dedicated to the Word of God. He was apparently a great godly leader for eighteen years simply following the words of prophets and what spiritual advisors led him to believe was God's will. But it wasn't until he found the Book and began to live by it that He truly became an exceptional leader for God. Where is the Book hidden in your leadership? In your meetings, in your plans, in your personal life, in your family, in your dreams, in your preaching and teaching? Find it. Look under the couch, if necessary. Find the Word and become a leader of the Book.

CHAPTER THREE

Solomon's Wish

"So give your servant a discerning heart to govern your people
and to distinguish between right and wrong. For who is able to
govern this great people of yours?" (1 Kings 3:9).

"I will do what you have asked. I will give you a wise and discerning heart, so that there will never have been anyone like
you, nor will there ever be" (1 Kings 3:12).

"God gave Solomon wisdom and very great insight, and a breadth
of understanding as measureless as the sand on the seashore"
(1 Kings 4:29).

Every minister has a wish list. If the proverbial genie in a
bottle were a reality and one suddenly appeared in the pastor's study, I'm sure most leaders could put together a
short list of wishes ready to fill. Of course, the list would vary from
leader to leader and day to day.

> "God's work of giving wisdom
> consists in choosing the best
> means to the best end. God's
> work of giving wisdom is a means
> to His chosen end of restoring
> and perfecting the relationship
> between Himself and men for
> which He made them."
>
> J.I. Packer, *Knowing God*
> (Downers Grove, IL:
> InterVarsity Press, 1973), p. 97.

The leader's wish on Sunday
morning would begin with a request
for the best sermon (or lesson) that
was ever preached. Or there may be
a request for just one Sunday without criticism from the usual crowd.
"Just one Sunday, I wish Miss Kiljoy
or Mr. Blankenbrain would just
walk on by without giving me input
on how things should be done." Still another wish may be for an
unusually large (record) attendance that would impress the people
and make the minister feel successful. Or better yet, a Saturday
night wish: "How about a blizzard that would cancel Sunday serv-

ices and give me a day of rest at home with my family?" The Sunday wish list certainly has some appeal.

On Monday, the wish list may change some. The leader is a little more battle worn and bleary-eyed come Monday morning. He spends most of his day shuffling through the leftovers of last week's to-do list, critiquing his own leadership failures from the day before, and noting the urgent issues this week's schedule brings. As the last gulps of some very strong coffee pass his lips, the Monday-morning leader has a definite cynicism. "I wish my critics would be put to public disgrace and apologize to me in front of the entire congregation as everyone, with tears in their eyes, begs my forgiveness." At the very least, one may ask for all of the week's problems to be immediately removed and thrown into the depths of the sea. Or at least one day without any phone messages, e-mails, and surprise appointments.

On payday, the desire may be for a raise. At conventions and conferences, the wish might be for some notoriety and a chance to lead the workshop instead of attend it. At the end of the year, the pastor may ask for a better year to come. During vacation he may wish for the sun to stand still and the vacation to miraculously be extended. In hard family times, he may wish for perfect kids and the model marriage. The young leader would wish for respect and the older leader may request the energy of youth. The list is virtually limitless. But this is only a dream. There is no leadership genie and there are no leadership wishes to be granted.

There was, however, a wish granted for king number three in the history of Israel. As he assumed the leadership role for God's people, the Lord Almighty (note: much more powerful and effective than your average genie) told the freshly anointed King Solomon that He would give him anything he asked for. In effect, the Lord was giving Solomon one wish. What wish would top Solomon's list? Perhaps a little background will help us understand his choice and be useful in our observation of God's leaders.

Solomon's father, King David, had been king for forty years. Even though he was a man after God's heart, he had a couple of things going against him. He was a man of war, who was constantly on the run and embattled from every side. Someone was always trying to kill David. He also had a less than desirable home life with many kids from several wives. He wasn't a great father (see chapter 9). A number of David's sons were interested in claiming his throne. Absalom had attempted a coup before David's death, and Adonijah made an attempt to usurp power as he was dying. But David loved Bathsheba and had promised her that her son would sit on the throne. With little difficulty, Solomon became king. He inherited a kingdom that was united, had virtually no enemies, and was beginning to prosper. If timing is everything, Solomon had it. His authority was unquestioned and his power was great. The historic record tells us, "The kingdom was now firmly established in Solomon's hands" (1 Kings 2:46). What more could he possibly need to be a successful leader?

Not long after Solomon's reign began, he went to Gibeon to make a sacrifice to God. This was not God's ordained location for

> The Tabernacle and the altar of burnt offering appear to have been on a hill in Gibeon even though David had brought the Ark of the Covenant to Jerusalem. (See 1 Chronicles 21:29.)

sacrifice. But this was quite an impressive sacrifice. It included a thousand burnt offerings on the altar there. Perhaps this kind of devotion and sacrifice stirred the very heart of God as He saw the son of David follow his father's footsteps of worship. Solomon's heart was right, even though he didn't do exactly the right thing. It could be that God saw great leadership potential and wanted to empower it. Maybe God had planned this dream sequence all along. We don't know exactly why God moved in this out-of-the-ordinary way, but we know he did. He appeared to Solomon in a dream and gave him one wish.

It appears that God may have expected a request other than the one He got. Scripture indicates that God was very pleased with Solomon's wish. God commended the young king for his choice. If Solomon had wished for prosperity and wealth, who could have blamed him? Many successful leaders are drawn in by

Follow God's Thread

When God appeared to Solomon in a dream, it was evidence of His concern for the everlasting throne of David. When God granted him superior wisdom, it displayed God's intent to bless His people through a wise leader.

the material possessions this world has to offer. If he had asked for long life, that would be entirely understandable since death is one of mankind's biggest fears. If he had requested curses and defeat on all of the surrounding nations and their kings, God wouldn't blame him. Solomon had seen his dad return from battle bloody, tired, and hungry. It was less than glamorous, and it certainly would have been logical to request military dominance.

But to God's cosmic delight, Solomon asked for something much more valuable than these. Here's what the Bible record reveals as Solomon's wish:

> Now, O LORD my God, you have made your servant king in place of my father David. But I am only a little child and do not know how to carry out my duties. Your servant is here among the people you have chosen, a great people, too numerous to count or number. So give your servant a discerning heart to govern your people and to distinguish between right and wrong. For who is able to govern this great people of yours? (1 Kings 3:7-9)

Of all the things this young king could have asked for (and remember God would have given him anything), he asked for wisdom. This is where today's leader goes to school. His choice must be our choice. If we are to be great leaders in the kingdom of God, it is going to require God's gift of wisdom.

But before we get to the practical ways a leader can grow in wisdom, we should note from this account how much God desires wisdom for people who would lead for Him. He does the typical God thing and let's us choose, but when we choose wisdom as a priority, He is elated with the choice. Why? Because when we choose wisdom, we have not only chosen a very important leadership trait, we have chosen a characteristic that is a direct reflection of who

> "For the foolishness of God is wiser than man's wisdom, and the weakness of God is stronger than man's strength" (1 Corinthians 1:25).

God is. In effect, the leader who chooses wisdom chooses to lead by God brains instead of human brains. God desires us to have this kind of wisdom. But how do we get it and how does this wisdom make us better leaders?

There are several ways to get wisdom, but the first point of this observation is that we must desire it. There must be a hunger for it that is deeper than the variety of other leadership appetites.

Remember the fictitious wish list of the pastor in the study at the beginning of this chapter? Frankly, many of these wishes might seem more pragmatic than a desire for wisdom. The mistake many of us make is that we desire the rewards of leadership without the discipline of wisdom. Even though we may never get a chance at the spiritual wishing well, our actions reflect what our true desires are.

Many of today's leaders prefer success, prosperity, and popularity to wisdom. Listen to the conversation of leaders you know and see if the conversation is filled with self-confident advice or humble listening/learning. Watch to see if there is much discussion about accomplishments or sincere questions focused on maturing. When you're with a leader, is the focus on the leader or the kingdom? What you will find is that many leaders are unlike Solomon in that they feel like they have it all together. They have either seriously overcalculated their own abilities or underestimated the challenge of leadership. Solomon had no such delusions. He felt incapable ("I don't know how to carry out my duties") and overwhelmed ("who is able to govern this great people of yours?"). These two attitudes contributed to Solomon's choice, and they can help us to seek wisdom also.

Wisdom begins here for the leader. The oft-quoted Scripture "to fear the Lord is the beginning of wisdom" (Proverbs 1:7) indicates that wisdom begins with an understanding that God holds it all together. There is no wisdom apart from Him. If we see our true selves, this will be an easy understanding. What Christian organization, local congregation, or dedicated ministry isn't overwhelming? What Christian leader truly finds himself capable in all aspects of leadership? This is why we seek wisdom, and it all begins when we take God seriously. God is never overwhelmed. God is always capable. To understand this is a wish for wisdom.

Wisdom continues for the leader when he understands that he is only a part of a grand plan. I believe this must be at least part of the Psalmist's thinking when he writes, "teach me to number my days aright, that I may gain a heart of wisdom" (Psalm 90:12). This wisdom verse comes in the midst of his discussion about how fleeting life is. It is a leader's realistic view that he has a certain number of years here to lead. After that, someone else will take his place. He is temporary.

This realization makes the leader wise for two reasons. 1) Wisdom comes to the leader who rightly measures his days because each day becomes an important learning opportunity, a chance to gain more insight and knowledge. 2) At the same time, realizing his limited time on earth teaches the leader to hope in something other than this life; it drives him towards eternal goals and helps him lead God's people there—very wise indeed!

"Yes," you may be saying, "but these are only philosophical thoughts about my desire to be wise." Does an adjustment in attitude alone cause someone to have wisdom? The answer is no. But without giving mental assent to the need for wisdom, a leader will never take the proper steps to get it. It will in fact only remain a wish. Desire for wisdom is only the beginning. There are definite steps to becoming wise as reflected by Solomon during his time on the throne.

We begin on the path to wisdom by asking for it. "If any of you lacks wisdom, he should ask God, who gives generously to all without finding fault, and it will be given to him" (James 1:5). Many leaders want to be perceived as wise, but never earnestly seek it from the Lord. From time to time (in emergencies when we have no answers) wisdom may find its way into our prayers, but not as consistently as it should. A true desire for wisdom will foster a conversation with God that asks for it all the time. There is no reason to believe that when God's leader asks God for wisdom, he is any less likely to get it than Solomon was. The beginning of Solomon's wisdom was that he desired it. Make a note of it. If he had asked for something else, he would not be known as the wisest man to ever live. But he wanted and asked for God's wisdom and the Lord granted it.

We continue to obtain wisdom by taking a stance of continual learning. Many leaders mistakenly assume that their education ends when they get a certain degree to decorate their wall. It appears that Solomon never stopped learning. The reality of leadership is

> Apparently Solomon continued his education well after God promised to give him wisdom. He worked hard at becoming even wiser and trying to understand as much as possible. (See Ecclesiastes 1:12-13.)

that learning should never end. Every event of every day of life is a classroom. Here is a phrase I happened across somewhere in my leadership journey which has deeply impacted me: "Let's go to school on this." This has become for me a kind of rule for life. It is often most useful following some blunder or failure but shows a desire to learn from mistakes. Leadership school is in session every day. This is why Bill Thrall, Bruce McNicol, and Ken McElrath, in their book *The Ascent of a Leader* (San Francisco: Jossey-Bass Publishers, 1999) advise us to "remain teachable and try to learn all the time" (p. 120).

> "Scholars are not certain when formal schools began to emerge in Israel. Schools may have been in existence as early as the time of David. . . . Archeologists have unearthed tablets inscribed with school exercises from that period."
> Jill Maynard, ed., *Bible Life and Times* (Pleasantville, NY: The Reader's Digest Association, 1997), p. 120.

For example, we can go to school on human relations. In the course of ministry, we may experience some staff problems because of some miscommunication. Of course, most of us can't relate. Christians always work together in perfect harmony and

> "Change and growth require teachability. To remain teachable, leaders can let go of their pride and let the other ordinary people around them provide input into their lives and decisions."
> *Ascent of a Leader*, p. 154.

never misunderstand. It's one big Jesus love fest when Christians form a team (if you don't recognize this as sarcasm, go take a nap and try this chapter later). For the rest of us who do experience miscommunication within our team that may lead to hurt feelings, jealousy, etc., this is an education opportunity—go to school and learn. What caused the misunderstanding? Why did this staff member perceive this or that? What new communication practice will prevent this from happening again? The answers to these questions become part of the leader's wisdom bank and make him wiser the next time.

While Solomon may have never struggled with staff relationships, he did show a desire for daily learning and ever-increasing wisdom. He went to school on everyday life situations. His judgment concerning the two women who both claimed the same child as their own was likely a part of his wisdom teaching. From that time on, he would know there is nothing like the love of a mother for her child. It was forever etched into his leadership-wisdom memory bank. Life, however, is not the only wisdom teacher.

The continual learning process is enhanced by reading. Many leaders read only to find neat quotes and illustrations for points they are trying to make. But this is not the kind of reading and studying that will make the leader wise. There should be a variety of books read every year (set a goal) that help God's man or woman become all that God desires.

A leader can grow in his leadership by reading everything he can get his hands on in the area of his passion and giftedness. Are you a preacher? Read about preaching. Youth minister? Books about youth culture would be good. Worship pastor? Read books, magazines, articles that deal with worship. This kind of reading makes you better at what you do, but reading only books in your passion area makes you dangerously one-dimensional.

Your reading might also include Christian classics to tap into the thinking of former great leaders. Leaders can read spiritual growth books to help them mature in their faith. Men and women of God may make fiction a part of their reading to spur creativity. Today's leader would do well to read Christian biographies to inspire and Christian history to find his place in the story. A great leader will read books that are culturally relevant so he can relate to the people he is trying to lead.

Aside from this, the leader can read books for leisure because he is, after all, a person who needs relaxation. From time to time, you may even read a book without underlining or highlighting— just for fun. This is reading for enjoyment and relaxation, but it is about gaining wisdom and insight from the thoughts and words of others.

I know the ideas listed above may make you feel like you just read the most oppressive syllabus in the history of education. There are so many books to be read, today's leader can't possibly read them all. But great leaders will find that discipline in this area will help them gain wisdom in all parts of life.

Finally, a learning tool that leaders often overlook is people. Most leaders could benefit from a mentor. There are a million lessons to be learned from an older generation of leadership, even if they are no longer in the trenches. If they've served God in a leadership capacity, they have some wisdom to share. Unfortunately, many attempt to lead without the wisdom of those who have gone before, but this is as foolish as Rehoboam (Solomon's son) who rejected the counsel of his father's elders and followed the brash advice of his friends. The result is frequently the same: leadership is jeopardized. So then, how can we tap into this living wisdom?

When you are in a group of leaders who have much more experience than you, speak little. If you speak too much, you'll sound foolish to those who have been where you are. They won't tell you how foolish you are, they will simply smile at each other and listen. Later, after years of experience, you'll hear a young leader spouting off about "how it should be," and you'll just smile and listen. But you'll know that you were like that once.

> "Everyone should be quick to listen, slow to speak . . . " (James 1:19).

On the other hand, if you will listen, you'll be amazed at the words of wisdom coming from the hearts of veteran leaders. Taking time to ponder their witness and counsel will help you form your own leadership traits internally without exposing your lack of understanding. These bits of wisdom can be used as leadership building blocks for you in the future.

To take this a step further, e-mail or call veteran leaders from time to time to get their advice. Most of us have older, wiser leaders we know who have great insights to many of the problems we are experiencing. A phone call that is respectful of his time (don't talk for more than five minutes) or an e-mail that is succinct (don't write an e-mail that's more than a couple of paragraphs) presents an opportunity for some quick wisdom. Tell the person you are calling that you respect the work he has done and that you would appreciate some insight into whatever issue you're facing. When he gives you an answer, thank him and end the conversation. He will feel good about helping a younger leader, and you will get some great advice.

The most intense way to learn from someone who's had experience is to approach a veteran leader and humbly ask him to enter into a mentoring relationship with you. Again, be careful to respect the value of his time and be specific as to what it is you are after. Most leaders are honored to invest in others in this way. After all, this one-on-one interaction is leadership in its most intense form. Don't approach someone to try to get close to him based on his title and how it will make you look. Spend time praying for God's guidance in this area. Then find someone who knows you <u>and will be able to give you good guidance. Don't ever</u> <u>be late or "just forget" to show up for an appointment. Don't</u> argue with his opinions—you are seeking <u>his wisdom. Come pre-</u> <u>pared with questions each time you meet. This keeps the mentor</u> <u>from having to keep the conversation going.</u>

Of course, the best way to gain wisdom simply can't be rushed. Life can be the best and most effective teacher of wisdom. Daily experiences and unexpected life twists have a way of making us wise over time. At the end of Solomon's life, he had written thousands of proverbs, hundreds of songs, and had understanding in plant life, animals, and people. He was by God's promise the wisest man that ever lived because of a wish. He chose wisdom.

You may never be thought of as wise, have a queen come to hear your lectures, or write a bunch of proverbs (do fortune cook-ies count?), but you can grow in wisdom. You can wish for it, pur-sue it, and by God's own word receive it. For God is pleased with the leader who above all else seeks wisdom.

CHAPTER FOUR

Worship Leading

"David and the whole house of Israel were celebrating with all their might before the LORD, with songs and with harps, lyres, tambourines, sistrums and cymbals" (2 Samuel 6:5).

"David, wearing a linen ephod, danced before the LORD with all his might, while he and the entire house of Israel brought up the ark of the LORD with shouts and sound of trumpets" (2 Samuel 6:14-15).

"I will praise you, O LORD, with all my heart; I will tell of all your wonders. I will be glad and rejoice in you; I will sing praise to your name, O Most High" (Psalm 9:1-2).

N o, this is not another bandwagon participant for more expressive corporate worship. We've all heard it before, haven't we? David entered Jerusalem with a live band, so let's crank up the guitars and rock for God. Not only was it loud, it was expressive. David danced before the Lord and raised hands of praise, so God's people should be demonstrative in their corporate worship times on Sunday morning. On top of that, he danced in His underwear (linen ephod), so there should be no dress code for church.

> "When an honest, humble soul comes to meet Him, Jesus can make Himself alive to us anywhere. Come. Sing. Love. Give. Listen. Don't Criticize. Smile. Praise. Look past imperfect people to God. Worship Him."
>
> Jack Hayford, *The Power and Blessing* (Wheaton, IL: Victor Books, 1994), p. 159.

This passage has been interpreted, misinterpreted, overinterpreted, overdone, overused, manipulated, and misused more times than you could number. But I don't want to talk about the musical worship experience at your church building on a given Sunday.

This is not a book about musical worship; but it is a book about biblical leadership. To be sure, this spectacular day of corporate worship (as recorded in 2 Samuel 6) was certainly a celebrative, spiritual mountaintop experience. It may rank in the top ten of all on-earth (sorry, the angels probably have us beat) attempts at adoring God. But it was also a leadership moment, for in this instance, the people worshiped under the passionate influence of Israel's greatest leader.

There is more than just a great worship service here. It's a look at the worship life of a man who had a heart in tune with God's. To be sure, David was the man who brought military superiority and stability to this fragile nation. He was a great fighter, but he was also the man who wrote much of the Jewish hymnbook. This account gives us a glimpse of this warrior/harp player in the middle of his personal adoration and celebration of God. You can see merely a corporate worship experience here, or you can see a leader at work. David was at his leadership best in this moment of intense public worship. He was leading worship.

By this time, David had already proven himself on the battleground. Many knew him because of his legendary defeat of the Philistine giant, Goliath. Some knew him because hit songs in Jerusalem proclaimed that he had killed his tens of thousands. Still others had followed his guerrilla tactics in En Gedi as he

> Early in David's career his army consisted of about 400 shady characters he gathered to himself as he was on the run from Saul. (See 1 Samuel 22:2.)

spent years with a ragtag army alternating between fighting Philistines and running from King Saul. Finally, after Saul's demise on the mountains of Gilboa, all the elders met in Hebron to anoint David as their new king. This was the official recognition of the anointing by Samuel many years earlier in Bethlehem. His first order of business was to attack the Jebusites and claim Jerusalem as his town. Then by the Lord's guidance he had come to defeat the Philistines soundly and reclaim domination over the territory where the ark of the covenant was being

> Hebron is south of Jerusalem and was originally called Kiriath Arba. It is the same town in which Abraham buried his wife Sara after purchasing a cave in the field of Machpelah. (See Judges 1:10 and Genesis 23:2-20.)

housed. Once again, the great general David had organized 30,000 of Israel's fiercest fighters into a well-oiled machine and brought victory to God's people. But soon he would lead them in a deeper, more meaningful way.

Let's pause for a moment and reflect upon today's church leaders. Have you ever wondered why so many of today's Christian leaders accomplish great victories for God but aren't embraced by their people as David was? Could it be that there is a deeper leadership the people of God need to witness in us that comes only when we lead them in worship?

What are we talking about here? It is the dreaded "What have you done for me lately?" syndrome. Leadership in the midst of "success" is easy. When the attendance is growing, people give credit to leadership. When the budget is under control and giving is up, criticism towards leadership is ignored. When the great plans and programs to reach into the community are met with participation and publicity, no one calls for the heads of leadership on a platter. When the church is growing, the sermons are direct revelations of God. When the organization is moving forward, the leader is a genius. When the building is completed and fully paid for, there are no inquiries into how decisions were made. People tend to follow blindly in the good times.

But leadership under these conditions usually doesn't last long. No matter how good a leader you are, there will be times (many times) when ministry feels like failure. There will be periods when the attendance doesn't soar. Offerings will not always exceed expectations. And programs will not always go off as planned. Truthfully, much of what we as leaders plan will fail. Staff hires that we initiate will prove to be poor choices. Ideas we promote will, in the long run, be viewed as simplistic. Programs we put all our energies into will amount to nothing more than wasted time. This is where leadership becomes crucial. What will cause the people of God to follow us in times like these? If God's people see in the leader a submissive life of worship, they will be more inclined to follow. Just something to ponder as we head back to Jerusalem to observe a king at worship.

One of the happiest consequences of the Philistine defeat was regaining control over the ark of the covenant. David immediately thought of this sacred furniture that represented the presence of

God as the centerpiece of his new town, Jerusalem. A great celebration was planned with full fanfare. A special carriage was built to bring the ark home, and the procession began with David leading the way. He was cel-

> ## Follow God's Thread
>
> The ark was symbolic of God's presence and power. Its presence powerfully indicated that God was moving in this episode of Israelite history.

ebrating the victory of his God with his people. But there was still a worship lesson David needed to learn.

Maybe the potholes were deep near Nacon's threshing floor. Maybe the oxcart was poorly made. Or perhaps the guys steering the ark were careless. Whatever the case, the oxen stumbled, the cart tipped, the ark leaned, and Uzzah instinctively reached out to steady it. You would think this was a very fortunate move. After all, an ark with one of the cherubim broken off isn't nearly as attractive. But Uzzah wasn't rewarded for his quick thinking on this day of celebration. Instead, God struck Uzzah dead for his irreverence. He had disobeyed the long-standing rule never to touch the golden seat of the Almighty. The music stopped. Worship service over. Let's all go home. And David sulked.

The fear that swept over David because of the day's events caused him to leave the ark at Obed-Edom's house for three months. The king returned home. The people wondered what this meant about David's relationship with God. And Obed-Edom received incredible blessing. David went back to the drawing board. He read up on how the ark should have been handled, and finally, he could stand it no longer. The urge to praise God for his victories, coupled with a new, healthy fear inspired him to organize another day of worship.

"Obed-edom was a Levite of the family of the Korahites . . . and belonged to the class of Levitical doorkeepers, whose duty it was, in connection with other Levites, to watch over the ark in the sacred tent."

C.F. Keil and F. Delitzsch, *Commentary on the Old Testament*, vol. 2 (Peabody, MA: Hendrickson, 2001), p. 591.

This time, plans were made to handle the ark correctly. The priests were carrying the ark. David offered sacrifices to the Lord before it. He personally led the procession into town with music and dancing and shouts of praise. David made a spectacle of himself that day, according to his wife who watched from the window. But he didn't care. On this day, David won as many leadership points as he ever had on any battlefield. He led the people to worship God because they witnessed his passion for the Almighty.

The apostle Paul stated the leadership principle that David exhibited. "Follow me as I follow the example of Christ" (1 Corinthians 11:1). This is an important lesson for God's leaders. They are first and foremost followers. Part of why people follow Christian leaders is that they have confidence that the leader is pursuing God. They believe that the leader has pursued relationship with Jesus to the extent that he can help them in their journey. That's why they follow.

Many of today's leaders skip this important lesson. As we have already mentioned, the topic and idea of leadership dominates seminars, books, and conferences for leaders. Thousands flock to these events seeking ways to become better leaders, but in the process forget that before anyone will follow them, they must follow Christ. It could be contended that many of the great Christian leaders in history were simply God-followers. They didn't understand how to value teammates or inspire volunteers. They followed Jesus and inspired others to come along on the journey. In the same way, this experience in David's life teaches us valuable leadership lessons even though that wasn't his focus.

First, David teaches us to be private in our worship. This is one leadership characteristic you can't fake. If the leader doesn't have legitimate times of worship and praise in all walks of life, then it isn't likely he'll be able to convince anyone on Sunday that he is sincere. If you don't pray (not just before meals and bedtime), your public prayers will become shallow and trite. If you're not a student of the Word, your preaching and teaching will lack passion and insight. The minister who never lays prostrate in his office will be hard pressed to feign humility during a worship service. The one who refuses to meditate on God during the week will never lead the people to do so. Those who want to have a lively celebration experience in public will need to practice in private.

His example also teaches the leader to set an example in a public way. Even though relationship with God is an intensely personal endeavor, the leader's walk is, of necessity, a public one. There is no planning for this, it simply happens. David was lost in worship as the ark followed him into Jerusalem. There must have been some ecstasy of the Spirit that caused him to shed clothes while he was dancing. In that moment the thousands who lined the parade route were unimportant. David was expressing love for God. But even as he danced before God, he had to be aware that everyone was viewing him as king. Today's leader is no different.

When the pastor goes to the store, there are people there who know him and watch to see if his actions and words match with his claims that Christ is Lord. When the youth pastor goes to the movies, teens take note as to what the movie is rated. The minister is under the proverbial microscope during prayer time, musical worship, communion, and offering. How we express our passion and love for God will either increase or diminish our leadership authority with the people we lead. After this day, the people of Israel put a high priority on corporate worship because their king did. When people see us pray or lift hands in worship or humbly bow in prayer, they believe that we are connected to a higher authority, and this allows them to trust us in a way they couldn't otherwise. If those who follow us do not see us in positions of humility before God, they will conclude we don't have relationship with Him. They may tolerate this in good times, but when the hard times come, they will dismiss us as unspiritual, power-hungry tyrants.

This lesson is simple. Learn to live lives of worship. Worship requires an object of adoration, a heartfelt devotion to that object, and an action or actions that reflect that dedication. In this case the leader must have an intimate heart-feeling toward God and structure his life in such a way that those who see his actions will recognize whom he loves. For people who witness this life of worship in the leader, following becomes very easy. They will want what the leader has. They will emulate the leaders' actions as the leader follows.

One more lesson is to be gained from this worship service led by the king. The people must witness the leader giving glory to God. Why was David dancing before God? David was getting "jiggy" to point to God. He was cutting a rug to honor the Lord. The king was doing a two-step that said, "God did this!" The point of the public display of affection was to let everyone know that God had been faithful. God had given them this city. The

Lord had defeated the Philistines. David's dance of worship was
giving credit where credit was due.

God's leaders must not miss this important fact. Anything
(and I mean anything) great that happens in the process of leading the people of God is a direct result of His providential power
and wisdom. Followers don't
always understand this. They
sometimes tell their leaders the
silliest things, "Only you could
open the Word that way." "I
don't know where this church
would be without you." "I owe
my salvation to you." "You've saved my marriage." "You are a
genius." Okay, no one ever told me I was a genius, but that's not
the point. The point is that many want to give the leader credit for
success. We are wrong to accept it.

> "Be careful not to do your 'acts of
> righteousness' before men, to be seen
> by them. If you do you will have no
> reward from your Father in heaven"
> (Matthew 6:1).

The temptation is to accept it. The temptation is to believe
that we really are pretty capable on our own. The temptation is to
say "it was nothing" on the outside, while the inner soul is scream-
ing, "give me more praise!" The foolish leader will allow such
compliments to go to his head. He will begin to believe that God
couldn't do the kingdom without him. But the great leader knows
better. The great leader will constantly work at pointing people to
God. He realizes his weaknesses and how incapable he is without
God directing every step. He dances in public, but his dancing
points to God.

Several years ago, our congregation had rented out the local
college arena for a special Christmas Eve service. We spent several
weeks planning for a spectacular, yet reverent presentation of the
birth of Christ. We were very blessed with a sizable attendance on
that evening, and the program went as expected. In my speaking
role, I had introduced the theme of the evening, and, of course,
there were carols to be sung and special music to be performed,
but the best part was reserved for the grand finale.

Toward the end of the service, our senior pastor was to give
a sort of devotional as a grand procession entered the arena to center court where we had constructed an elaborate stable. As all the
characters came to the Christ child to worship, Gary continued to
tell of the wonderful events of Christ's birth. By the end of his

speaking the typical Christmas characters were kneeling before the baby Jesus. The wise men were there with their gifts of gold, frankincense, and myrrh. Several shepherds were there bowing with staffs in hand. Mary looked peaceful and Joseph stoic. The ox and lamb kept time (you get the picture).

The program called for a big musical worship number to end the evening. This is where our senior pastor made an incredible leadership gesture. He walked over to the stable and in his Christmas sweater and slacks, he knelt before Jesus. Gary is a respected leader. For many years he has led our congregation and been an influencer in our community. His peers know him as an innovator and thinker. But as he was caught up in the moment, he went away from the script and assumed a humble position at the manger.

I suppose, most of those in attendance that evening will never know what I knew. His kneeling wasn't what the programming team had planned. He was simply supposed to walk out of the spotlight as the music began. But instead of leaving, he bowed down. And when he knelt, the rest of us were compelled to do the same. The vocalists knelt. The worship leader knelt. Some of the band members knelt. People in the arena seats knelt. I was overcome with a sense of God's greatness as I sank to my knees. It was a worshipful experience. I was kneeling not because someone had asked me to, but because I had seen it. Our leader led us to worship the King. It's the lesson of king David's public dance.

CHAPTER FIVE

Driven

"The driving is like that of Jehu, son of Nimshi—he drives like a madman" (2 Kings 9:20).

"Jehu said, 'Come with me and see my zeal for the Lord.' Then he had him ride along in his chariot" (2 Kings 10:16).

O ne of the most interesting kings in the history of Israel was a wild man by the name of Jehu. He came to the throne totally by God's design. God had chosen him to be leader, even though Jehu didn't see it coming. He was God's man for fulfilling his prophecies about the destruction of the royal-but-wicked house of king Ahab. As we will see, he was certainly called in an amazing way. What's more remarkable, however, is the incredible passion that is ignited in the heart of this army officer turned king! From the moment he realized that he had been set apart, he became passionate about being God's leader for this job. Examining the Bible record in 2 Kings 9 will help us better understand and apply his story.

> " . . . the soul refuses to be harnessed; it knows nothing of Day-Timers and deadlines and P&L statements. The soul longs for passion, for freedom, for life."
>
> John Eldredge. *Wild at Heart* (Nashville: Thomas Nelson, 2001), p. 6.

Two of Ahab's relatives, Ahaziah, king of Judah, and Joram, king of Israel (Ahab's son), had joined forces to war against the King of Aram. Unfortunately for them, the battle wasn't a success. As a matter of fact, Joram was seriously injured in battle and had retreated to Jezreel to recuperate. His troops remained in Ramoth Gilead, more than 30 miles to the east, beaten, tired, and awaiting new marching orders.

On one of those days, as some of the officers sat around telling war stories, a prophet from the company of Elisha appeared. He was out of breath from running to this camp, and he was carrying a flask of oil. You must remember that, at this time in Israel, the prophets of God had taken a

> According to the chronology of the kings he served with, Elisha was God's spokesman for 60 years.

backseat in prominence and influence. They were always warning of impending doom and the need for repentance, and they were generally disrespected. Frankly, most people considered them to be eccentric and harmless, if not crazy.

It was in this context of spiritual apathy that a prophet appeared and interrupted the conversation with a request to speak with one of the commanders (Jehu) alone. Since the prophet said it was important, Jehu obliged, and they made their way into the tent. No sooner had they closed the flap behind them than that prophet opened the flask and poured oil on the head of Jehu. He spoke on behalf of the Lord and anointed him king of Israel. He charged him by God's word to lead a campaign to completely eliminate the house of Ahab. A short time later the prophet tucked his cloak into his belt and bolted

Follow God's Thread

The thread of God had been sewn into Jehu's heart long before his calling. Earlier, Jehu had been riding his chariot alongside king Ahab when he overheard Elijah's words. The prophet foretold the day when Ahab's own flesh and blood would die in Naboth's field and when it happened, Jehu remembered. (See 1 Kings 21:19 and 2 Kings 9:25.)

from the tent for his return trip home. Meanwhile, a freshly oiled Jehu emerged from the tent thoughtfully stunned.

The other officers immediately questioned him, "What did that wacko want?" The remarkable thing is that Jehu initially tried to act as if nothing had happened. He had just been charged with a leadership role, and he wasn't sure he wanted to take it. He simply responded by saying that the prophet was crazy and always saying something strange, and this time was no different. It has always amazed me that Jehu thought that would be the end of the discussion and that no one would question the oil dripping down his face from his hair. It appeared for a moment that he was going to ignore the anointing and call to be king and simply return to being an officer. But his buddies pressed him and he finally told them the whole story.

These leaders must have been ready for change, for they acted as soon as he told them that God wanted him to be king. They blew the trumpets and humbly laid down their clothes to declare, "Jehu is king!" The adventure was underway. Over the next two chapters, Jehu and his army went on one of the most horrendous killing sprees in the history of hostile takeovers.

They began with the wounded king Joram in Jezreel. This is where we first get an indication of what kind of guy Jehu was. Under his leadership, the troops formerly under the command of Joram sped towards Jezreel. As they approached the city, the watchman couldn't tell who was coming, but he guessed who it might be by the reckless driving style. "The driving is like that of Jehu," he answered in reply to the king's inquiry. Jehu was known for driving like a madman! God knew this trait in Jehu and purposed to use it for His glory.

Two messengers were sent from the city on horseback to meet the fast approaching army and were told to ask if they came in peace, but both times, the messengers fell in behind this madman and became a part of his army. Finally, Joram in his weakened state and his relative Ahaziah, king of Judah, made their chariots ready and went to meet this company on their own. As they approached, they too asked if Jehu came in peace, but they soon realized he wasn't there to talk. He drew an arrow and hit Joram between the shoulders as he fled. Ahaziah temporarily escaped, but later died from an injury Jehu's men had inflicted. Both kings were dead according to God's plan, but Jehu wasn't finished.

He continued towards Jezreel, and as he entered the city, he made his way to the tower searching for Jezebel. She was arguably the most ungodly woman ever. She had almost single-handedly led Israel in an extreme, evil idolatry. She prided herself on her powers of seduction, so she painted herself, batted her eyes at Jehu, and asked if he had come to kill her, too. After securing the allegiance of some eunuchs standing next to her, he told them to throw her down. They obliged, and the wicked queen mother was dead, her blood splattered against the wall. All this killing was making Jehu and his men hungry, so they went inside and had a feast. While they were eating, Jehu did consider giving Jezebel a queen's burial, but when they went outside the dogs had completely devoured her. God had prophesied this exact form of death and humiliation for Jezebel, but Jehu wasn't finished. There was more work to be done.

From his newly established headquarters, Jehu sent word to Samaria to inform the leaders of the city of the death of the two kings and to have them appoint one of the seventy sons (which could mean any male relative) to succeed Joram as king and for them to defend his crown. The leaders of the city decided that they couldn't defeat a guy who had already overthrown two kings, so they agreed to kill all the natural heirs to the throne and send their heads in baskets to Jehu in Jezreel. This eliminated all the male descendants of Ahab as God had foretold, but Jehu's mission was still not complete.

Next he prepared his chariot and headed north to Samaria (driving like a crazy man as usual). On the way, he met some relatives of Ahaziah's at a local shepherd's hangout. When he found out they were related to Ahab, he killed forty-two of them on the spot.

Continuing on his journey, he came across an obscure man of faith named Jehonadab. He screeched his chariot to a halt and asked Jehonadab if he was in accord with him. What do you say to a man who has blood on his hands and a fiery glare in his eyes? "Yes!" Jehu invited Jehonadab into the chariot (hopefully the chariot had an air bag and seat belts!) and

> Jehonadab was a devout man who apparently had instructed his family to abstain from drinking wine, building houses, and planting fields. (See Jeremiah 35:1-10.)

encouraged him to come and see his zeal for the Lord. They made their way up to Samaria where Jehu feigned loyalty to Baal, and when he had gathered all the prophets of Baal together in their temple, he had them executed. In this way, Jehu accomplished God's plan for wiping out a wicked king's family and the evil idolatry that they had brought to Israel.

But what value could this Bible story possibly hold for us? What leadership lesson can be learned from this reckless chariot driver? What attribute did he have that made him such a good leader for God on this holy rampage? What gave him the focus necessary to complete this incredible holy rampage? In a word, it was "zeal." Jehu was driven when he drove his chariot, and he was driven spiritually by his passion for God. Before we talk about how this passionate drive can benefit us as leaders, let's define exactly what it is.

The Hebrew word that is translated "zeal" in 2 Kings 10:16, is found forty-three times in the Old Testament record. It is a word that has to do with passion, anger, and envy, but it is mostly about jealousy. As a matter of fact, the word that Jehu uses to explain the "why" behind his actions, is most often translated "jealousy." More specifically, this word describes a heart which burns to defend the Name of God. Jehu used this word on his way to Samaria to identify his personal passion with God's passion. God was jealous for the love that His people were giving to the false god Baal. Jehu wasn't just killing Ahab out of a selfish desire to have his throne. No, his heart beat for the true God of Israel whom Ahab's family had profaned with their idol worship. But what does this mean for leadership in the church?

As a pastor or church leader gains years of experience in leading a congregation, there is a definite tendency to lose passion for the ministry. Over time a church leader sometimes learns that the best way is to not make waves but to just go through the motions. It is much easier to placate difficult people than to confront them. It is fairly easy to be there when someone in the flock goes into the hospital, loses a loved one, has a baby, needs some counseling or gets married. The years of weekly teaching and preaching preparation can become routine and dull. Decision making at board meetings becomes a rubber stamping session for safe, less than ambitious plans. In a word, we as church leaders often become complacent.

The sad thing is that most of us had zeal at one time. We had a calling that burned deep in our soul, some kind of eternal purpose that drove us. But now we are tempted to simply go through the motions of a weekly routine hoping that no one will notice our boredom and that somehow God will show up and do something. However, our expectations are low that even God will make something happen. The radical plans to change the world have long been abandoned for nice-sounding church-speak that will make everybody happy. Often, the leader doesn't even know it's happened. We have simply learned how to avoid being hurt again—we are surviving. <u>Needless to say, when the church leaders have lost their passion, the people who follow suffer.</u>

At first glance, it would seem unimportant that a church leader doesn't have a fire in his belly and glazed look in his eye when he speaks of Kingdom stuff. Does today's church leader really need to drive the chariot called "church" a little like a madman at times? After all, not everyone is cut out to be Mel Gibson painting their faces for war, and yelling, "Freedom!" Is it so wrong to drive safely? Is it a bad thing to take the old advice that 90% of life is just showing up? Can't we as leaders just show up? There are three scriptural teachings that tell us, "No."

The first reference is found in the last book of the Old Testament. In the first chapter of the book of Malachi we find the spiritual leaders of Israel going through the motions. God reprimands the priests who serve at the temple for bringing blemished sacrifices, having contempt

> Malachi was the final prophet of the Old Testament era, whose ministry is dated around 450–400 B.C. He prophesied to God's people who had reinstituted the temple and many religious practices after their captivity, but whose hearts were apathetic.

for the priests' portion of food from the altar, and sniffing at the incense contemptuously. They were just showing up. They were fulfilling all the requirements of the law in the physical sense, but <u>their hearts were not in it. And what was God's verdict for these passionless priests? The answer is found in Malachi 1:10,</u> "Oh, that one of you would shut the temple doors, so that you would not light useless fires on my altar!" God did not like the lack of zeal these leaders exhibited, and I wonder if there aren't times when He would like to shut the doors of our churches as we go through the motions of leadership?

It was four hundred years later and also in the temple where we find our second teaching about going through the motions. Jesus had just begun His ministry. He was off to a good start, turning some heads down in Cana with some refreshment help at a wedding He was attending. A short time later, Jesus made His way to the temple for the

> Cana was the hometown of the apostle Nathanael.

Passover celebration and a chance to worship His heavenly Father. But when He arrived, the joy of worship was sucked right out of

Him as He witnessed the disrespect taking place in His Father's house.

In an instant, he was flipping tables and driving animals away. This wasn't a time for subtlety! He was making a statement and people noticed. What happened? Did He just have a bad day? Did the disciples say something wrong? Doesn't Jesus like animals? None of the above. What caused Him to react this way? Zeal! John 2:17 says, "His disciples remembered that it is written: 'Zeal for your house will consume me.'" Jesus had such a passion for God that He wanted to make a statement. There was something wrong going on in the temple, and a burning welled up in the Savior's heart until it burst forth in action. I can only guess what He would do in some of our meetings when people say or do unholy things in the name of God.

Finally, did you know that you and I are commanded to have this passionate drive as we serve God? Romans 12 is famous for that quote about "living sacrifices," but verse 11 is also a word that every good leader should take to heart, "Never be lacking in zeal, but keep your spiritual fervor, serving the Lord." You and I have a mandate from Scripture to do more than just show up! God calls us to face the challenges of leadership with a passion that drives the programs we promote, the decisions we make, and the dreams we dream. The leadership displayed in the life of Jehu will be our guide to this kind of passionate leadership.

First things first. If you want to be a leader, you must make sure you are a leader. This thought may not make sense until it sinks in. The question we must all ask ourselves is, "Has God called me to lead?" The second one is like it, "How has He gifted me to do so?" For Jehu this was easy. A prophet showed up one day and anointed him as the next king of Israel. Wouldn't it be nice if all church leaders were appointed by prophets of God? Wouldn't all of us feel a little more confident if we approached our jobs on a daily basis knowing that we're doing exactly what God had designed us to do? Well, a prophet may not run up and ask to see you in the tent, but without a calling you will not be able to lead with zeal.

Most leaders have moments of depression and doubt. Anyone who has ever tried to motivate others has questioned whether or not he has what it takes to lead. But the thing that drove Jehu and the thing that must drive today's leader is a knowledge that God has called him to the task. If you are not sure that God has called you to lead, don't expect anyone to follow; but if you know down deep that God has a directive for you to accomplish, get in your chariot and go; others will be right behind you!

This is the second part of understanding your appointment to lead—finding how God has gifted you to do so. For Jehu, it was easy. He apparently liked to drive chariots hard and fast. He would be the one at the stoplight revving his horses (literally) to challenge someone to a race. He liked to fly down the dusty road with the wind blowing in his hair, and that's exactly the kind of guy God needed for the job of wiping out the wicked royal family. Jehu was called to lead, and he led in a way that fit him perfectly.

This is part of the challenge to leading with zeal. Many pastors spend years beating themselves up for what they are not. They are constantly trying to become more organized, more dynamic, more outgoing, more humorous, more administrative, etc. . . . Why don't we just spend time trying to discover how God has woven our lives together to make us who we are and lead as He has designed? Passionate leadership comes from leaders who are confident, not in who they are, but in who God has molded them to be. When we truly believe that God has called us to lead and has uniquely gifted us to do so, we will lead with zeal. Why? Because the

> *Why don't we just spend time trying to discover how God has woven our lives together to make us who we are and lead as He has designed?*

enemy of zeal is timidity, and who can be timid when God wants you to go on a wild chariot ride? To be sure, knowing that you are called to lead is part of the battle, but Jehu had more.

Great leaders don't hesitate. Have you ever been to a Damon's restaurant? It's great food, with big screen TVs and a trivia game. If you request a trivia game box from your waiter, you can actually compete against other restaurant patrons to see who has the most knowledge. The game is played by choosing the right multiple choice answer quickly. The sooner you punch in the letter that corresponds to the right answer, the more points you get. As time goes by, a series of clues comes onto the screen and you can usually get the answer by a process of elimination, but points decrease as time increases. This illustrates an important leadership lesson. Sooner or later, everyone knows the answer, but those who act on it first get more points.

Jehu had a slight moment of hesitation when he came out of the tent, but when his fellow commanders heard what the prophet said and proclaimed him king, he acted. Zeal propels us forward. Zeal moves. Jehu didn't take his time getting to Jezreel; he got his chariot ready and went immediately. Jesus didn't hesitate; when He saw unholiness in the temple, He started throwing tables.

When God calls you to lead, He wants you to move ahead. Many church leaders have great ideas and plans and visions for their congregations, but they are hesitant to share them for fear they will be rejected. The zealous leader says, "I'm going to kill the kings and destroy Baal worship, so let's go." The zealous leader says, "I'm going to bring change to the way we worship corporately, so let's go." The zealous leader says, "Let's do something different that will help us win people to Christ." The zealous leader moves and asks others to join. He knows the time is now.

Let's pause and ask ourselves this question, "What would have happened if all of the men or some of them had not followed Jehu?" We don't know, but I'm betting he would've ridden to Jezreel alone, for he was on God's mission. When you know God is doing something in your heart and wants to do something where you are, don't wait. Do it now.

Observe how Jehu completed the task. It wasn't enough for Jehu to kill Jehoram and Ahaziah. It wasn't enough to kill the seventy princely heirs to the throne. It wasn't enough for him to kill the prophets of Baal. Jehu completely eradicated the king's family and Baal worship. Many church leaders are definitely called, and they jump in with both feet, but when the going gets tough, they get discouraged and quit.

Where did we ever get the idea that leading would be easy? Life wasn't easy for any Bible leader. Moses didn't have it easy when two to three million people and all their animals were thirsty.

> "There is always risk. There is always sacrifice. But it is an individual's willingness to break through the barriers imposed by risk and sacrifice that positions him or her to see what could become a reality. He who shrinks back from the challenge spends his life wondering."
>
> Andy Stanley, *Visioneering* (Sisters, OR: Multnomah, 1999), p. 127.

Paul didn't have it easy when people stoned him for his teaching. And Jehu didn't have an easy time of accomplishing his task for the Lord. It was hard-driving, mentally stressful, and physically demanding work, but he didn't stop until every descendant of Ahab and every prophet of Baal was gone. What work did God lay on your heart days ago, months ago, years ago? Don't you think you should finish it? Pull out those old plans, dust them off, and get to work on them right away to the glory of God.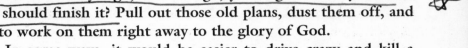

In some ways, it would be easier to drive crazy and kill a bunch of wicked people, but God has called us to something much more special. He has called us to get rid of the wickedness of this world by connecting people with Jesus Christ. If you've been called by God to be a leader in His church, then you are a part of His plan to eternally change the lives of people. There is no greater calling. It makes your heart beat faster. It pumps spiritual adrenaline throughout your soul. This calling brings a glimmer to your eyes, a hop to your step, and fire to your veins. Your sermons hum. Your meetings are daring. Your plans are monumental. You are consumed with zeal for God. Like Jehu, you are driven!

CHAPTER SIX
Heart for the Helpless

"'Don't be afraid,' David said to him, 'for I will surely show you kindness for the sake of your father Jonathan. I will restore to you all the land that belonged to your grandfather Saul, and you will always eat at my table'" (2 Samuel 9:7).

"So Mephibosheth ate at David's table like one of the king's sons. And Mephibosheth lived in Jerusalem, because he always ate at the king's table, and he was crippled in both feet" (2 Samuel 9:13).

"Religion that God our Father accepts as pure and faultless is this: to look after orphans and widows in their distress. . ." (James 1:27).

There is a place far away from the spotlight. The filth and smell of the place may possibly disgust or literally sicken you. The people here demand patience, understanding, and effort. Excuses to avoid this place will come easily. There will always seem to be something more important on your "to do" list. You often go with an attitude of unfortunate obligation and just as often leave feeling guilty for having felt that way. Far from accolades and applause, spiritual leaders learn important lessons here. To skip these places and these people is to miss the point entirely. Let's go visit a nursing home.

As you pull into the parking lot, you are muttering to yourself in a nearly audible voice,

> "As long as we are occupied and preoccupied with our desire to do good but are not able to feel the crying need of those who suffer, our help remains hanging somewhere between our minds and our hands and does not descend into the heart of where we can care."
>
> Henri Nouwen, *Out of Solitude* (Notre Dame, IN: Ave Maria Press, 1974), p. 45.

"Can't wait 'til this is over." The front door opens as usual and you encounter that smell (it's a bit stereotypical, but true, if you've ever been to a nursing home, you know what I'm talking about). The faces of the women and men dressed in white are friendly but tired. They hustle from room to room in a constant flurry of activity.

Other than the workers, you are surrounded by helpless people. Many of them can't walk. Most of them can't go to the bathroom, bathe, or feed themselves. Some of these people can't communicate. Still others communicate with loud incoherent groanings and curses. You make your way to the familiar place at the end of the east wing where you find the 85-year-old charter member of your congregation. In her prime, there was no one who could play the piano like her, but now she sits sideways in her recliner, paralyzed on one side as a result of a stroke suffered several years ago.

You enter the room with a greeting, but you receive no response. You get closer and look into her eyes. Her hair is a mess and she is drooling, but her eyes are still alive with recollection and understanding. So you spend the next fifteen minutes having a one-sided conversation about your church services that morning. You give the condensed version of the sermon, sing one or two hymns, and mention the people who were there. Finally, you offer communion. After preparing the juice and the cracker, you pray thanking the Lord for His sacrifice and push the bread to her lips. She reflexively eats. You gently hold the cup to her lips and pour as much as you can into her mouth. Much of it dribbles down her chin. After a few more comments of "we love you" and "we're praying for you" you head down the hall.

The pace quickens as some people shout from their independent ghettos begging you to come back—a man in a wheel chair is following close behind and gaining on you. As you leave the stale air and exit to the outdoors, the fresh air hits you almost as abruptly as the stale air had when you had entered. You open the car door, plop into the driver's seat, and put the key into the ignition. Before cranking the engine, you pause. In spite of all the negatives that assault you when you start out, there is something right about this experience. There is probably nothing you dread each week more than heading to the nursing home to serve communion, but there is nothing that brings as much satisfaction. You feel close to God. You leave a better person, and even though you were alone, you grew in leadership.

> "The King will reply, 'I tell you the truth, whatever you did for one of the least of these brothers of mine, you did for me'" (Matthew 25:40).

This hypothetical visit to the nursing home is one of many situations where the church leader is called to spend time with the helpless. It is only one of many other places and people: the cancer ward in a hospital, the emergency room, a funeral home, and homeless shelters. In these places we find kids in poverty, people who don't want to live, parents who have lost control, and spouses who have been betrayed. These are places where people are helpless. These are leadership places without the accolades. The people here don't care about your title or your accomplishments. There is only one question that matters, "Can you help?"

This discussion about leading the helpless brings us to the throne room of King David in Jerusalem. As long as twenty years may have expired since he had conquered this former Canaanite city of Jebus and made it his own. He must have had a break in the action. No Philistine threats. No reports from the front lines. Kids not fighting. Tired of writing psalms. In this kingly lull, something caused him to remember his good friend Jonathan who had perished in that battle long ago. The question of the day: "Are there any relatives left in the house of Saul?" David was looking for a cousin, a brother-in-law, even a nephew. Any relative would do. He simply wanted to show kindness to his best friend Jonathan by caring for a member of Jonathan's family.

> The last time David had seen Jonathan was in a place called Horesh in the desert of Ziph as David was fleeing from Saul. (See 1 Samuel 23:16-18.)

After contacting one of Saul's former servants, David learned that indeed, there was a relative that remained alive. This was a bit unusual since the first action of most kings in this time was to wipe out the entire family of the former king, thus eliminating any possible claim to the throne. But because of the quick thinking of a simple household servant, one of Jonathan's sons, Mephibosheth, was still alive. His nurse, upon hearing of Saul and Jonathan's death, quickly led the young boy out of the palace into hiding. Unfortunately, in her haste to save his life, he fell and was from that point on, unable to walk. He was lame in both feet.

Now, twenty years later, this former prince had a family and lived in obscurity in the house of a wealthy merchant. Unable to work and care for his family, he relied on the generosity of his host. His life was less than glamorous and maybe a bit humble, but he was alive and had a family and food to eat. And then out of the blue, this helpless cripple was summoned to see the king of Israel at once. He must have shuddered in anticipation of such an encounter. Why would the king want to see him? Was he planning on finally killing the last living link to Saul's throne? What could he possibly offer the king?

> ## Follow God's Thread
>
> God graciously kept Mephibosheth alive and provided for his needs by His grace. Perhaps He kept Mephibosheth alive to give David the opportunity to express his heart for helpless people. David's care for this cripple perfectly illustrates God's desire for us to care for those who can't repay our kindness.

> The name "Mephibosheth" literally means "getting rid of the idol." He was also called by the name of Merib-baal. (See 1 Chronicles 8:34.)

We don't know the scene in the throne room that day. The Bible doesn't give us the details, but we can guess. Did Mephibosheth enter in a crude wheelchair? Was he carried into the king's presence by servants? Or was he able to slowly hobble into the great room with the aid of some crutches? His entrance wasn't important, his reception was.

The king jumped from his throne at the sight of Mephibosheth. This man's legs were unsightly and shriveled, but his face bore a strong resemblance to his father's. The young man must have hesitated as this leader of leaders approached. But the compassion coming from David's eyes convinced him it was an act of mercy that motivated him. They embraced. David wept for his friend Jonathan as he said, "You look just like your father." Mephibosheth was overwhelmed. And then David announced his intent. "Because of my love for your father, all of your father's lands are restored to you, and you will be my personal guest at every meal here in the palace until the day you die."

Here is leadership: the king with the former prince turned pauper; the physically limited dining with the strong; the poor eating at the table of the rich; the great and the small; the leader paying attention to the needs of the helpless. There is much here for today's leader to take in.

Great leadership for God must have an understanding of His heart for the helpless. God always made provision for the helpless. Orphans and widows were of special concern to Him throughout the entire Old Testament as law after law provided for their care. The things that stirred God to anger most were those things that took advantage of the underprivileged. The actions that He noticed were those acts of kindness to someone in trouble. Indeed, His entire salvation plan was based on the helplessness of people lost in their sin. That's why He referred to us as lost sheep who have gone astray. It is in our helplessness that God's love is made perfect. Today's leader must care for the helpless because God still cares for the helpless.

> One of the final curses Moses delivers on God's behalf has to do with people who prevent an orphan or widow from getting justice. (See Deuteronomy 27:19.)

Scholars have often debated what it actually means when the Bible says that David was a man after God's own heart. I believe that his compassion for the helpless is a major part of it. This descendent of Saul had nothing to offer. He couldn't work. He couldn't give gifts. This young man wasn't beautiful to look at. He didn't look royal. He wasn't going to promote David's fame. He couldn't ride with him into battle. He couldn't even walk on his own. He was helpless. And David helped him. He not only helped him, he honored him. And this is where the great leaders find themselves—caring for helpless people. Even James, the brother of our Lord, taught that the best kind of religion before God was to care for orphans and widows. They are the epitome of helplessness, and the person who serves them with nothing to gain for himself is a man after God's own heart.

Today's church leader needs to be concerned for the helpless. The plight of the homeless should stir a sadness that leads to action. Building relationships with mentally or physically handicapped people needs to be a common occurrence. Real godly leaders give of their personal resources to help those who need money or clothes or food. God's men and women willingly offer support and time to those who are sick and destitute. Why? Because God cares for the helpless and a leader can never lead people to God without developing this compassion in his own heart.

Great leadership continues by following the example of Jesus with concern to the helpless. Look carefully at the ministry of Jesus. What kind of people took up His time? Where do we most often find Him? What did He spend most of His days doing? The ministry of Christ was with people in need, touching them where they hurt the most, bringing wholeness into their lives. The ministry of Christ was about helping people. Look at the most desperate groups of Jewish society that Jesus restored.

Lepers were helpless people. They were physically and socially cut off from everyone and everything. They couldn't touch or be touched. Those inflicted with this disease were removed from their family. There was no cure for leprosy and there was no hope for lepers—until Jesus came along. When Jesus came to town, lepers were acknowledged, touched, and healed.

The adulteress was a helpless person. She was condemned by the law of Moses and the very Word of God because of her guilt. The religious used her, glared at her, accused her, and judged her. The crowd laughed at her, ridiculed her, and picked up stones to throw at her. Her situation was helpless—until Jesus came along. When Jesus rose to address her, she was given dignity, forgiveness, and a chance to try again.

> "Stoning was the most common form of capital punishment prescribed by Israelite law. Executions usually took place outside the city, after at least two witnesses presented evidence. The accusers were required to throw the first stones at the convicted person. . . . "
>
> Jill Maynard, ed., *Bible Life and Times* (Pleasantville, NY: Reader's Digest Association, 1997), p. 334.

The widow in Nain was helpless. Her son was dead and this grief-stricken lady followed the procession to the burial cave with tear-stained cheeks and swollen eyes. She had been here before. Same road. Same dirge. Same people. Same pain. Same helpless feeling. Only this time, it was her son instead of her husband. Who could help her now? Widows looked to their sons for financial support, but now this particular widow did not have that option. We know from cultural historians that this woman would be destitute without the help of others. Jesus was walking that way and motioned to stop the death march. In the midst of this devastating experience, Jesus gave this woman strength, hope, joy—and he brought her son back to life.

The people God's leaders are called to guide are helpless. At some point God's children feel physically destroyed and socially cut off. They experience cancer, heart attacks, strokes, and broken bones. Like the lepers, they are left out feeling lonely and empty by those who are physically whole. This world is made up of guilty people. Caught time and time again doing the wrong thing and failing in their quest for the spiritual, they live life waiting for the condemning thud of stones to bring what they deserve. We are surrounded by those who are hopeless because they haven't figured out the questions of life and death. Great leaders for God use their gift of leadership to be Jesus to these people. Our visions must be dictated by how we can bring Jesus into their world. Our plans should be driven by the needs of these people. Our time needs to be spent bringing help to the helpless, for in doing so we bring the healing of Jesus into a hurting world. This is the objective of all godly leaders.

One more thing. . . . There is another similarity between David's story and ours that bears mentioning. The throne room is a lousy place to find helpless people. David was halfway into his forty-year reign at the time of this mercy call for Mephibosheth. He had spent much of this time in the trenches (or in his case, caves) of leadership. He had paid the price. He had been on the run. He had fought against all odds. The responsibility of many men and their families had weighed him down. But leaders, especially successful ones, have a tendency to forget the caves when they get the crown.

When everyone is waiting on you hand and foot, bowing in your presence, and addressing you as "Lord," it's really hard to stay grounded. When you are eating the best food and wearing the finest clothes, it doesn't take long to forget where you came from. It's only a matter of time before the place you used to know well becomes repulsive to you. Leadership can easily lead to feelings of superiority and invincibility. This is the final purpose for having a leadership heart for the helpless. It reminds us.

David gave Mephibosheth a lifetime pass at the king's buffet because of his love for Jonathan. But I think he also needed a visual of life in the real world. Every time this son of his best friend limped into the dining hall, David could see. Whenever David asked his guest to pass the salt, he noticed. For the rest of his royal days, a helpless person shared his bread, and David had a daily reminder of how helpless we all really are.

It is in the routine of our royal lifestyle that we sometimes forget our purpose as leaders. Often after years of ministry, we try to avoid encounters that are time- and energy-intensive with people who are in need of large amounts of grace. It's much easier to sit in a comfortable office, make plans, study for sermons, and lead the strong. But we need contact with helpless people to remind us. We can never forget that if no one were helpless, there would be no need for salvation, no need for a savior, no need for a church, no need for leaders.

Wherever you minister and whatever your leadership status, now would be a good time to reflect. Leadership in the kingdom is a high calling, but you can't stay in the throne room (even if it is just a poorly furnished office with old paneling and outdated furniture) basking in your authority. Step down from the throne for a minute. Remove the robe and set the crown aside. Put the throne phone on "do not disturb" and reflect. How often do you touch the helpless? How much time do you spend with those in need? How do you use your power to the advantage of the powerless?

Perhaps you need to ask a question not unlike the one David asked on that fateful day, "Is there anyone I can show kindness to?" The pastor, elder, or lay leader who asks this question on a daily basis will find God leading him to people who need help. When God leads you to these people, help them, serve them, invite them to supper. The spiritual reality will begin to leave its imprint upon your soul as it must have David's. We are all helpless, crippled guests, and we've been given the privilege of eating at the King's table.

CHAPTER SEVEN

Sticks and Stones

"As he cursed, Shimei said, 'Get out, get out, you man of blood, you scoundrel!' . . . The LORD has handed the kingdom over to your son Absalom. You have come to ruin because you are a man of blood" (2 Samuel 16:7-8).

"It may be that the LORD will see my distress and repay me with good for the cursing I am receiving today" (2 Samuel 16:12).

"So David and his men continued along the road while Shimei was going along the hillside opposite him, cursing as he went and throwing stones at him and showering him with dirt. The king and all the people with him arrived at their destination exhausted" (2 Samuel 16:13-14).

Some well-meaning mom started this whole thing. I'm sure it happened when a kid came home from school crying because someone had called him fat, stupid, or ugly. What's a mom to say? "Names can't hurt you, Sweety. Words can't break your bones, only sticks and stones can do that." With renewed encouragement the child returned to school the next day only to be insulted again. Only this time, instead of tears, the words flowed: "Sticks and stones may break my bones, but words can never hurt me."

> "Our natural response to criticism is to defend ourselves. This is especially true when our vision is under attack."
> Andy Stanley, *Visioneering* (Sisters, OR: Multnomah, 1999), p. 151.

Surely, he became a grade school cult hero that day. Not since "liar, liar, pants on fire" and "cross my heart, hope to die" had a young man expressed himself so eloquently. The expression shamed those who insulted him, and he became the most popular kid in school. But even though this imaginary kid's words have been quoted by thousands of children since, it doesn't mean that his words are true. Oh, it's true that words can't break bones, but they are capable of breaking the spirit. In fact, harsh words can hurt anyone to whom they are directed. Anyone who has ever felt the painful sting of a critic's words knows this to be true.

Hurtful words come in many different forms, but for a leader they come most often in the form of criticism. Of course, there is "constructive" criticism which can actually be helpful if it comes from someone you know and trust. Not to say this criticism is fun, but it can be useful if given in the right way.

> "One of the great downfalls of leaders is letting their egos hinder their effectiveness. They shield themselves from any form of criticism, so they foolishly quarantine themselves from wise counselors who could give them healthy advice."
>
> Henry and Richard Blackaby, *Spiritual Leadership* (Nashville: Broadman and Holman, 2001), p. 184.

In leadership there is also uninformed criticism—potshots from those on the fringe of your leadership world who don't know or understand. There always seems to be that person who rarely comes and is minimally involved who likes to say "I told you so" at the annual congregational meeting. As a leader ages, this kind of criticism actually seems to get a little easier to take as we are able to write it off as ignorance.

We can also face decision criticism. This type of criticism happens simply because as leaders we make hundreds of decisions on a weekly basis. How much should we increase the budget? What staff changes need to be made? What phone messages are a priority? What will be highlighted in the annual report? Should we close the office because of the impending snowstorm? What sermon series will be preached in February? What color should we paint, carpet, or tile? Leaders attempt to make the decisions that are best for the church and get others to follow, but doing so inevitably brings criticism. No matter what you decide, someone would have increased it more, chosen someone else, made different calls, given a different report, preached a different sermon, and painted a different color. The only basis for the criticism is a difference of opinion. But again, these words aren't too painful. They fall more into the category of disappointment than discouragement.

This leaves us to discuss the kind of criticism King David received. Spiritual criticism deals spiritual leaders the most devastating blow. These are the words that call into question our relationship with God, our leading by the Spirit, and our walk with the Lord. This criticism either comes at our lowest moments in ministry or quickly takes us there, and it drives us to mental, spiritual, and physical exhaustion. Anyone who has ever assumed a leadership position in the kingdom of God can relate to King David as he led his weary troops out of Jerusalem. He was on the run . . . again. And he faced the harshest of criticism yet.

An estranged Absalom had returned to Jerusalem and been united to his father the king. But David didn't know that Absalom was making a bid for his throne. For over four years Absalom had, unbeknownst to David, intercepted every person coming to Jerusalem for justice. He lied by saying that the king had no time to hear their cases, but that if he were made judge in Israel, he would see that everyone got justice. In short, he was running for office. He was at the end of the Jerusalem road shaking hands, kissing babies, and making promises. Second Samuel 15:6 says that he stole the hearts of Israel.

After he felt he had enough support, he asked his father's permission to go to Hebron to fulfill a nonexistent vow. His real intent was to call together an army and overthrow his father's kingdom. Upon his arrival, he blew the trumpet and the people shouted, "Long live king Absalom!" Thousands of fighters from all over Israel were gathered to him and ready to march on Jerusalem.

Meanwhile, back at the palace, David received word from a messenger that his son was up to no good and that he was advancing with an army to take David's throne. Pause for just a moment and reflect on the hurt David felt at the betrayal by his son. He had just shown him mercy by sparing his life for the murder of Amnon. Leaders often experience the same feelings of betrayal. You can help someone one day and the next he is ready to remove you from office. But David didn't dwell on this sadness too long. His survival instincts took over, and he prepared his men and all of their families to flee the city. Imagine packing up all the essential kingly stuff and leading this extensive entourage into the desert. They crossed the Kidron Valley and moved up the Mount of Olives where they sacrificed to God and wept for their misfortune. After instructing the priests to return the ark of God to the city, David led this weary, frustrated, and scared group of people out of the danger of Absalom's advancing army.

During Josiah's reign, the Kidron valley was the place where common people buried their dead. It therefore became known as an unclean place. Jesus crossed this same valley on the night of His betrayal as He made His way to Gethsemane. (See 2 Kings 23:6 and John 18:1.)

Life was at an all time low for the kingdom of David. He was not getting any younger. His nation was still relatively new and apparently unstable. His family was in harm's way. His son wanted to kill him. Could things get any worse? Enter a man by the name of Shimei.

Follow God's Thread

The king offering a sacrifice on the Mount of Olives points to a day when the King of kings would spend the night there contemplating His impending sacrifice for the salvation of all mankind.

By the time they had reached a place called Bahurim, it was late afternoon. They were plodding through a narrow pass when they were suddenly pelted with rocks and dirt from a cliff above. As they were showered with debris, the angry voice of one of Saul's distant relatives echoed through the valley. "You're a jerk David. You kill everyone you see. You have no mercy. Get out of town, you murderer. God is paying you back for all the evil you have done." The angry words spilled from his lips and fell on David's entourage like the rocks he threw.

The first reaction of many of David's men was, "Let me at him." Abishai was especially eager to put an end to this man's mouth. With drawn sword, he asked for the king's permission to chop his head off. You or

Abishai, Joab, and Asahel were nephews of David by his sister Zeruiah. Abishai was the oldest.

I may have sent Abishai on a mission to silence such a bold critic, but not David. In what was arguably one of his most discouraging leadership moments, he decided to take the tongue-lashing. He and his people marched on, as Shimei cursed and threw stones all the way.

The scriptural account notes that David's people were exhausted by the time they reached their destination. As David lay in his tent aching from the journey, he must have prayed what many godly leaders have thought if not uttered. "God, here I am. I don't know why this is happening to me. None of the things Shimei said are true. It hurts. But my trust is in You." Wondering what the next day would bring, David gave way to his weariness and slept.

This impromptu camping trip didn't last too long. As predicted Absalom came to town with full force. He humiliated the king by sleeping with his harem on the palace roof and then he sat on the throne in Jerusalem. But David had insiders who told him everything his adversarial son was planning and doing. With the help of God the whole coup came to a halt in a bloody battle in the forest of Ephraim. Twenty thousand rebels died at the hands of David's men, and his enemy son was killed by his commander. He came back to Jerusalem stronger than he had been before. He had endured the criticism and won the victory.

There is justice when an unjustified criticism comes to nothing. It's great when the plans that God births deep in our souls come to pass. It's exhilarating when you take a leadership step of faith and God comes through in a mighty way. There is nothing more incredible for a leader to weather the storm and be the last one standing. But the criticism was a part of it all, and it will return. There is no one who ever tried to do something for God that wasn't criticized.

Moses was criticized when the Israelites had to make bricks without straw, and he lived to lead his people out of Egypt. Nehemiah was told that rebuilding the wall of Jerusalem was an impossibility, but he stood on top of it when it was done. Gideon was laughed at when he told three hundred men they could defeat thousands, but he had the last laugh. The apostles were ridiculed as being drunk when they spoke in tongues at Pentecost, but it was no joke that 3,000 were baptized. Silas may have questioned Paul's idea to sing when they found themselves in a Philippian jail, but their faith brought an earthquake of change to a jailer's life. Even Jesus was taunted and mocked as the king of the Jews, but someday every knee will bow. It's not *if* you will be criticized as a leader for God, but *when*. So what can we do with it when it arrives?

When criticism comes, the first thing is to find out whether or not it's true. Sometimes criticism can cut because the words ring close to home. First, you must ask God to show you if there is any truth to the criticism. If there is, you must ask God's forgiveness, and then apologize to anyone you have offended. It may be helpful to talk with trusted friends in times like these. Recount for them the situation and the words cast against you. Let this neutral person help you understand if you need to repent.

Observe how David handled this criticism from Shimei. Many leaders have a tendency to lash back when someone hits them with harsh words. It would have been natural for the king to trade insults with Shimei, or throw rocks back at him. We certainly would have overlooked it if David had ordered his death. But he didn't jump to any conclusions. He actually talked about letting God take care of the justice of it all. Many times in ministry, we find ourselves filled with pride and a desire to vindicate ourselves. But this is not the example David gave us. When we are criticized in our leadership, there is wisdom in putting off a response.

But what if the criticism is unfounded? Many times the leader will consult his mentors and friends, and spend much time in prayer and come to the conclusion that the words spoken against him are untrue. This calls for a loving conversation with the accusing party to explain things and seek unity. There are many times when this act of peace will bring out repentance and reconciliation on both sides. It is biblical to take a third

> "But if he will not listen, take one or two others along, so that 'every matter may be established by the testimony of two or three witnesses'" (Matthew 18:16).

party to hear both sides in these instances. Interestingly enough, as David returned to his city, Shimei presented himself face down before the king begging his forgiveness. The king granted it and spared his life. Even though criticism causes much pain in a leader's life, we are called to spare our critics' spiritual lives with grace and mercy.

In its ugliest form, criticism sometimes does not reach the leader's ears until it has reached many others in the form of gossip. This kind of criticism, true or not, can be devastating to a leader's reputation and therefore his ability to lead, especially when it calls into question his spirituality. It is one thing to be criticized for being stupid, but it is another to be labeled as someone who does not follow God.

Shimei's criticism of David was as devastating as it could be.
He said David was a man of blood. This was true. God confirmed
this part of David's character as the reason he was not allowed to
build God a permanent house. David knew this to be true. His
hilltop critic also accused him of wrongly killing Saul and taking
his throne. This was not true. David had many opportunities to
kill the former king, but would not raise a hand against him.
David knew these words to be false. But it was the final slander
that hurt David the most. Shimei claimed that God had departed
from him and was actually causing all of this to happen to David
as punishment. This was too much for David to bear.

This is the struggle for any leader whose spiritual integrity
has been called into question. We begin (like David must have) to
question ourselves. Maybe I am in this for me. Maybe I don't follow the Holy Spirit enough. Perhaps my ego or pride is in the way.
Do I really not care for people the way I should? Maybe my prayer
life does stink. And as more and more of our followers are infected with these judgments on our
souls, we lose the ability to lead.
This is where leadership for God
differs from corporate leadership.
Corporate leaders can lead even
when their moral life is in shambles. Their title gives them this
privilege. But when the spiritual leader's walk is questioned, leadership is gone.

> "As a visionary, the one thing you can control and must protect at all costs is your moral authority."
> Andy Stanley, *Visioneering* (Sisters, OR: Multnomah, 1999), p. 180.

This is the time when we need to get away from it all. David
reached his destination and was refreshed. When we receive the
heaviest kind of criticism, there is an important destination that
calls: anywhere but here. Sometimes a leader loses perspective in
the middle of the battlefield. He needs to retreat and get a different view. Only in this time of renewed commitment and soul-
searching will the great leader survive such trying times. It is in
these times that we have to come back to one realization.

God knows the truth. He always has and He always will. He
knew that David was fleeing because of the wicked schemes of his
son. He knew David would return to the throne. And God knows

when we receive hurtful words. He knows our hearts. He knows how it will all turn out. He has full understanding of the criticism that is being leveled against us. Somehow, this knowledge allows God's leader to keep leading when all seems hopeless. It is a great leadership trait to keep going when the critics' arrows are whizzing by. This is when the leader trusts God more than ever—to change his weaknesses, to bring justice, and to continue to help him lead.

> "Blessed are you when people insult you, persecute you and falsely say all kinds of evil against you because of me. Rejoice and be glad, because great is your reward in heaven, for in the same way they persecuted the prophets who were before you" (Matthew 5:11-12).

When the rocks and dirt start flying in your church, you, as the leader, have three options. You could quit. You could give in to the pressure of criticism and walk away. Many leaders take this option only to find the same Shimei in a different location. If you don't quit, you could throw rocks back. Of course, many pastors, elders, and lay leaders choose this path and campaign right back against their critics. This is a never-ending battle of words that brings disunity to the Lord's church. Or you could follow the example of David. Sometimes God's leader simply walks on, focused on his God and his calling knowing that there is a destination where he will be refreshed.

I wish that I could tell you that criticism is a rarity in the ministry. But of course, that would not be true. As I write this chapter, I can say that I've never had a broken bone, but I have been broken by the words of those who have criticized me. And if you have led for God, you and I could compare notes. But we take hope in the fact our critics' words are not final, God's are. He has said he will use our weaknesses to do strong things. He promises to use our stupidity to do smart things. Through Jesus, He has called us to an integral part of His eternal kingdom, and because of these eternal truths, we can change the old saying to "words can never hurt us forever."

CHAPTER EIGHT

Distractions

"King Solomon was greater in riches and wisdom than all the other kings of the earth. The whole world sought audience with Solomon to hear the wisdom God had put in his heart" (1 Kings 10:23-24).

"The weight of gold that Solomon received yearly was 666 talents, not including the revenues from merchants and traders and from all the Arabian kings and the governors of the land" (1 Kings 10:14-15).

"Solomon accumulated chariots and horses; he had fourteen hundred chariots and twelve thousand horses, which he kept in the chariot cities and also with him in Jerusalem" (1 Kings 10:26).

"King Solomon, however, loved many foreign women besides Pharaoh's daughter—Moabites, Ammonites, Edomites, Sidonians, and Hittites. . . . As Solomon grew old, his wives turned his heart. . ." (1 Kings 11:1-4).

Spiritual leaders don't walk away from God all at once. This is not to say that leaders in the church don't end their careers by chilling pulpits and board meetings with cold hearts that once were warm with Christ. It is to say that the process of moving from God to something else is rather gradual.

Many times we see only the end of this process. When someone in Christian leadership fails morally, people take notice. The misdeeds of some pretty popular religious leaders have been well documented. These well-known failures have made the word "televangelist" synonymous with "fraud" or "phony" in

> "It seems the higher leaders climb, the lonelier they become, hiding their true passions and personal challenges from others."
> Bill Thrall, Bruce McNicol, and Ken McElrath, *The Ascent of a Leader* (San Francisco: Jossey-Bass, 1999), p. 20.

much of our society. Who can forget the accusations against and the public arrest of Jim Bakker as the PTL empire imploded? What about the allegations and subsequent televised repentance of Jimmy Swaggert? The church still feels the effect of these misdeeds years after they occurred. Of course, this kind of thing is repeated on a smaller scale in

> "I had once thought that God had abandoned me. I thought my days of ministering for the Lord were done. I thought that I would never preach again. I was wrong."
> Jim Bakker, *I Was Wrong* (Nashville: Thomas Nelson, 1996), p. 632.

local congregations with all too frequent regularity. Like the church of Ephesus in Revelation 2, it is apparent that many preachers, teachers, elders, lay ministers, and parachurch executives just seem to lose sight of their first love.

The question is "why?" Most men and women who lead in the church are called to lead, gifted to lead, and passionate about doing great things for God. And yet many of them end up wandering from their calling, floundering in their leadership, and avoiding the faith risks that once drove them. What causes this dramatic transformation in once great leaders? What goes on from calling to falling? What's the deal between A and Z? What turns God's leaders into adultery, idolatry, selfishness, greed, pride, materialism, etc. . . ? In a word—distractions.

The church I pastor has a stage with a loading dock which makes moving heavy equipment and props for our special productions and weekly services a lot easier. It is really a great convenience, and it is hidden to those in the audience by a series of large, theater style curtains. This allows us to set the stage for the weekend services behind the curtains while we do something else in front of them.

One Wednesday night, I was preaching at our midweek service and I heard some clanking behind the curtains. This was not good for me. My surroundings can easily distract me from my thoughts and I was distracted! Another second passed and the sound of wind was heard along with the sight of these heavy curtains being blown by the gusts. Now the people were distracted, so I made some crack about the Holy Spirit sweeping through and then began to look behind the curtains to see what was going on. Our music pastor rushed backstage to see if he could help and I was generally playing with the situation, joking with the audience.

In less than half a minute the blowing curtains had stopped, but I was totally lost. I didn't know where I had been in my notes or what point I was trying to make. So I did what any experienced speaker would do—I stared blankly at the crowd and asked, "Where was I?" A lady in the front row hollered, "FOCUS!" She wasn't reprimanding me. She was reminding me of my fourth and final point on my outline, "Focus." It was a humorous experience. I had perfectly illustrated what happens when you lose focus.

What was going on backstage? Our worship leader told me later that the Sunday morning worship band was getting ready to rehearse for the upcoming weekend service. They had accidentally left the loading dock door open on a very windy night. This led to my preaching distraction. This is a picture of the leader's life. Distractions make it hard to focus. The more the distractions, the more out of focus things become. The more out of focus things become, the more leaders fail. There is not another leader in Scripture who illustrates this more perfectly than King Solomon. He had about as many distractions as a person could have.

You'll remember that Solomon was the king who requested wisdom, and God gave it to him. He became the wisest man to ever live. And along with the wisdom came some things that eventually distracted him from being a great leader. He started well, but by the end of his life, he found himself far away from the God whose house he built.

The book of 1 Kings spends the first eleven chapters telling the story of this great leader and his forty-year reign as king in Jerusalem. It was certainly a remarkable life. He would have without a doubt been featured on *Lifestyles of the Rich and Famous*. If he was a hip king, he would have made an appearance on MTV's *Cribs*. Solomon was the picture of prosperity at its most self-indulgent.

His kitchen activity alone gives some indication of his enormous wealth. Solomon had such a large number of officials working for him that he had a huge all-you-can-eat, Jerusalem palace buffet prepared every day. This included lamb chops (a hundred lambs), steak (twenty cows), and goat meat stew (a hundred goats) along with homemade bread (several bushels of flour and meal). I have no idea what they made with deer, gazelles, and roebucks, but you can be sure it was the finest cuisine of his day, and his chefs served up all these dishes on a daily basis.

But food was only the beginning. He had an embarrassment of possessions. Every king or queen who strolled into town brought gifts. Fine jewelry, horses, gold, silver, clothes, and trinkets were included in nearly every procession. I'm sure there were days when the king leaned back on his LazyThrone and yawned, "Oh, just what I wanted, more gold." He had thousands of horses and a city full of chariots. Want to travel by sea? He had ships. Need some gold swords or shields? He had a collection. Interested in some nice cedar furniture? His porch was stacked with it. Would you like to see some exotic animals? He had baboons, apes, and peacocks in his garden zoo.

Solomon had it all. He was so rich that silver became worthless. How worthless? In his day when you went into the Jerusalem convenience mart there was a dish by the cash register that said, "take some silver, leave some silver." Silver was as plentiful as the rocks on the ground!

Of course, Solomon was also very smart. This means he spent much of his time writing and speaking wisdom. The brilliance just flowed from this king. So, when he wasn't making legendary judgments (pretending to cut the baby in half to see who the real mom was), he was writing proverbs (not just the books we know of, but a collection of 3,000 wisdom sayings) and creating music (1,005 songs to his credit — his father would have been proud). On top of that, he could carry on an intelligent conversation on plant life, animals, birds, and fish.

Solomon's palace was the original Disneyland. Diplomats and royalty from all over the world came just to see and hear him. "Say something smart," they would challenge. And he never disappointed. That means that he had to carve out some time every day to think, "He who plots evil will be known as a schemer." Now Proverbs 24:8 may not seem too incredibly smart to you and me, but it's better than most fortune cookies, and he was cranking out these sayings on a daily basis.

Not only was Solomon advanced in both wealth and knowledge, he was also experienced in architecture, landscaping, and horticulture (fancy word for planting and growing things). He was a luxury home contractor. His first client was God. How do you build a house that makes the Almighty feel at home? Well, you build it exactly as He tells you to. Solomon gave this project his full energy and resources. He designed and was head foreman for this dwelling that took seven years to build. Then when he had finished with the temple, he built his house which took almost twice as long to build (13 years). He spent half of his reign building two houses. But he designed other things as well.

He headed up the "Beautify Jerusalem" campaign. He planted vineyards, gardens, and parks all over town. He planted fruit trees and designed and constructed reservoirs to water these trees. No doubt he improved the roads and had nice yards for all of his houses. When someone rode into the town of his father David, he would have marveled at almost everything that caught his eyes. This leader made civic pride possible through his many projects and improvements.

But possessions and achievements were not the biggest distractions for Solomon. Ultimately, it was his relationships that distracted him most. He had relationships with all the other kings of his day. He was friends with the king of Egypt. His good friend Hiram, king of Tyre, gave him all the wood for his houses, and Solomon gave him some cities. He hung out from time to time with the Queen of Sheba. Solomon's role as king brought him into long-distance relationships with the leaders of the known world.

Solomon also had relationships of an intimate nature. Many of his wives and concubines were given as gifts. Many kings gave him their daughters. But did he really need 1,000 women in his life? The official count was 700 wives and 300 concubines! You can only imagine some of the conversations around the palaces (he had several). "It's been six months since I've seen you . . . uh . . . er . . . what's your name again?" "Can you get these kids out of the throne room, I'm trying to be wise." "You love the other 999 better than you love me." "Were you thinking about me when you wrote *Song of Solomon*?" Relationship responsibilities must have overwhelmed him at times!

Fortunately, Solomon didn't have one of the distractions that his father had. He never really faced the prospect of war. No invading armies ever threatened the homeland. He was never in charge of a battle strat-

Scripture does mention two enemies Solomon faced. Both Hadad and Rezon were leaders of small armies that caused Solomon minor trouble, but neither was a real threat to the security of his kingdom. (See 1 Kings 11:14-25.)

egy. He never led troops heroically. He didn't have to negotiate treaties of peace. It's a good thing the Lord granted Solomon and the Israelite nation peace because this king didn't need any other distractions.

Distractions. Peripheral concerns that make us lose sight of what's important. Anyone who has ever led is susceptible. If you asked most leaders to name their number one purpose for existence, they could probably tell you what their focus should be. However, if you continued by asking how much time they spent on that one thing, you would find that many times the distractions get in the way.

Back to our king example. What one thing was he cut out for? What one gift did God endow him with above all others? God made Solomon wise. Ultimately, it was his extreme God-given wisdom that made him who he was. Why, then did he spend so much time with wives, architecture, zoology, and investments? I believe it's because as he increased in his influence, he neglected his gift, the thing he was made for—wisdom. After all, how wise was it to marry 700 women, spend more time building his palace than the house for God, or spend lavishly on the finer things of life? The point is, if it can happen to Solomon, it can happen to us. His story makes us aware of three major distractions in the leader's life.

The first distraction every leader faces is prosperity and the material gains that come with it. Now many of you may be thinking, "Ministry hasn't made me rich. I barely have enough to pay the bills." It's true that leadership in the church doesn't promise a whole lot of money, but on the other hand, it's not too bad either. Most churches and parachurch organizations have come a long way in the area of compensating pastors. Many receive a decent salary package including health care, retirement, disability, continuing education, and expense accounts.

Besides this, the pastor, in many settings, benefits from the generosity of the people he or she serves. Many times my family has been blessed with gifts of money, restaurant gift certificates, books, and entertainment. Often, people in my congregation will buy my lunch or breakfast. They are also generous with me in other things. I know of some leaders who have been given cars, boats, golf clubs, clothes, free medical services, club memberships, and vacations.

Don't get me wrong. God's leader is not prohibited from making a comfortable salary, and the encouraging gifts from the people who follow him are a true blessing from God Himself. The warning is not to let them become a distraction to ministry. At some point, it appears that Solomon forgot about being wise and focused more on how much gold he would get in a year, or what gifts some ambassador may lay at his feet. If it was not a temptation for us, Jesus would not have warned us so much about it. He knew that you cannot serve two masters. One will only distract you from the other.

The Christian leader can easily fall into the subtle trap of materialism. It happens like with Solomon when your house becomes bigger and demands more attention than God's house. When 401(k)s, raises, and major purchases begin to thrill us more than guiding people in God's direction, we have become distracted. When God appeared to Solomon in the dream, the young king wanted nothing more than wisdom. It was his prize possession. I wonder if the same could be said after thirty years on the throne.

The second distraction that we must carefully monitor is people. This may seem like a strange leadership proposition; after all, the people in our care are the whole point. If you take away people, there is no need for a leader. Paradoxically, these same people can become the distraction that renders the leader ineffective. This happens when the focus of the leader moves from God's calling to the "urgent needs" of the people. It's like a sign in a principal's office I once saw, "There they go and I must follow, for I am their leader."

Solomon lost focus in part because of his unhealthy relationships. The Scripture says he loved many foreign women. As he loved the women and catered to their concerns, he lost sight of God's plan. He ended up building altars, temples, and various places of worship to false gods. All because of the influence of his wives. Could it be that many of today's leaders end up building churches and organizations that cater to the desires of the people, but miss the mark with God?

> *Could it be that many of today's leaders end up building churches and organizations that cater to the desires of the people, but miss the mark with God?*

The leader must pay attention to people. A good leader will hear what they say, will understand what they feel, and will listen patiently, but will never waver in his focus. This means that good leaders work at guarding their calendars from those who would fill them up with the trivial. Pastors and leaders get bombarded with requests for meals, weddings, counseling sessions, meetings, organizations, and emergencies that arise. These will come in never-ending succession, and it is up to the leader to sometimes say, "No." The key is putting God's priorities on your weekly, monthly, and yearly schedule. This begins with identifying those priorities that God has for your life. This may include family, use of a spiritual gift, or a specific calling God has laid on your heart. Mark these down and don't let anyone steal your focus from them.

> "The key for overworked leaders is to examine each of their current responsibilities to determine whether they have inadvertently assumed ownership for things God has not intended for them to carry."
>
> Henry and Richard Blackaby, *Spiritual Leadership* (Nashville: Broadman and Holman, 2001), p. 203.

There is one other warning concerning distracting relationships. The leader can sometimes get so close to certain people within his organization that their opinions are given unfair access to information and decision making. It is a very powerful thing to sleep with a king, and that's why Solomon's heart was turned. It is potentially just as dangerous for close friends of leaders to weigh in on decisions. Friendships in Christian leadership are what it's all about, but the good leader will not let the relationship distract from making the right decision.

Finally, popularity can become a distraction to effective leadership. You can't tell me that the repeated, "Solomon, you're the wisest man I've ever seen," didn't have an effect on the king. He was probably, *Jerusalem Times* "Man of the Year" many times over. Everywhere he went, people bowed down to him, threw gifts, and praised him. Does this sound like your ministry?

Okay, maybe people don't bow down and constantly refer to you as wise, but they do have a tendency to put you on some type of spiritual pedestal. One of the incredible things that happens between leaders and followers is the expression of intense loyalty and respect. I've found that most people put me in a spiritual place that is unrealistic. It is important for the leader to take every praise to heart. For most it is a sincere display of gratitude and respect. However, the moment the leader begins to believe he is as good as people say, he is being distracted from God, the only One who really is good.

Follow God's Thread

God's thread through Solomon's life was His continued wisdom exhibited through the king. Even though history recorded that he had turned his heart away from God, Solomon still penned this famous passage that pointed young people to the Almighty. (See 1 Kings 11:1-6.)

Towards the end of his life, this wise king took note of these distractions in the book of Ecclesiastes. Solomon evaluated his entire life by reviewing the things he poured himself into. Besides saying they had all become meaningless, he pens some advice for would-be leaders.

> "Remember your Creator in the days of your youth, before the days of trouble come and the years approach when you will say, 'I find no pleasure in them'" (Ecclesiastes 12:1).

Don't lose sight of God. Don't be distracted. Don't let the peripheral dictate the direction. If you do, you will end up far away from God surrounded by applause of men but not producing kingdom-building results. Observe the life of this king. Learn from his mistakes. Listen to his advice. After all, he was the wisest man who ever lived!

CHAPTER NINE
Palace Life

"But Rehoboam rejected the advice the elders gave him and consulted the young men who had grown up with him and were serving him" (1 Kings 12:8).

"In everything he [Jehoshaphat] walked in the ways of his father Asa and did not stray from them; he did what was right in the eyes of the LORD" (1 Kings 22:43).

". . . Jehoram son of Jehoshaphat began his reign as king of Judah. He was thirty-two years old when he became king, and he reigned in Jerusalem eight years. He walked in the ways of the kings of Israel, as the house of Ahab had done, for he married a daughter of Ahab. He did evil in the eyes of the LORD" (2 Kings 8:16-18).

"Manasseh was twelve years old when he became king. . . . He did evil in the eyes of the LORD, following the detestable practices of the nations the LORD had driven out before the Israelites. He rebuilt the high places his father had destroyed. . . " (2 Kings 21:1-3).

There is something special about being the child of a church leader. It is both a blessing and a curse that everyone in the church knows everything about you. On one hand, they take care of you, and take you under their wings as though you were their very own. Although it's not always obvious and hard to understand at the time, most ministry kids are supported by the people who follow their parents. In most cases these people would do anything for the pastor's family.

> "And [the leader's] relationship management skills are most convincingly demonstrated within his family. Here is where a leader's true character comes through."
>
> Dr. Lynn Anderson, *They Smell Like Sheep* (West Monroe, LA: Howard Publishing, 1997), p. 144.

I was the son of a preacher-turned-elder. My dad was always a church leader as I was growing up, and I know that I received some special love because of it.

On the other hand, there are some pressures that come from being the child of a leader. Many times, the people of the congregation take it upon themselves to discipline you. They watch you when you talk during prayer. They see every wrong attitude and action and are more than willing to report it to your parents. It seems that there is an unwritten standard of behavior for all children of leaders within the church. It often comes to light through condescending phrases like, "I would have expected more out of Pastor Holy's son." Of course this is totally unfair, but it goes with the territory.

There are also experiences that only pastors' and elders' kids get to participate in. The best privilege is having the run of the building your parent works in. Church buildings are incredible places for games and adventure. In the churches I grew up in, I was familiar with every nook and cranny in the building. I knew where the communion preparation room was, which means I ate a lot of holy bread and drank a lot of sacred grape juice. I spent entire services under the pews, performed several piano recitals in the sanctuary (just banging on the keys, I was no child prodigy), and, yes, I swam in the baptistry. The children of leaders grow up with an all-access pass to a building that many consider holy ground. To the pastor's kids, it is both sacred and recreational.

Growing up in the leader's home also brings exposure to top secret information and in-depth analysis of certain people. The details of church politics spill into the back seat of the car in hushed whispers on the way home from church. "Mr. and Mrs. Johnson are struggling with their marriage." "The elders (or deacons, or Sunday school teachers, or volunteers—or a combination of all of them) are not doing their job." "The giving is down and the church is going to have to cut back." The observant kid could learn a lot about the people his mother or father work with. Sometimes it would be better not to know, but that doesn't seem to stop the information from flowing.

Above all, the children of a leadership home have a view of the church leader that no one else has. To everyone else, the pastor is the spiritual rock. But at home he's just Dad. To the congregation he is paid to give time. But at home just a few minutes of attention would be greatly appreciated. At work, everything is an emergency of eternal proportions because it's God's work. But at home, the kids just want to be a priority sometimes.

The leader's family gets to see the whole show. They see the friendly accommodating church smile and the impatient, grumpy morning rush. They witness the flowery Sunday morning language and the common, everyday slang. Even though the church sees the pastor dressed professionally and all together, at home the socks have holes and the shoes smell. The children are the ones who get a true picture of the leader as a person, and that is a very influential impression.

Some kids who grow up in ministry homes follow in their parents' footsteps becoming great leaders for God in their own right. Others reject not only their parents' leadership path, but their faith as well. Still others find themselves somewhere in the middle, neither embracing nor rejecting their religious heritage. They are left both embarrassed and proud to be a part of the holy family.

Like pastors' kids, most of the kings' children probably enjoyed palace privileges and also put up with royal standards. They were known as "prince" or "princess," and they were expected to measure up to their family legacy. They probably played hide-and-seek in the palace and were waited on by personal servants. Some of them turned out like Dad, and some of them were extreme opposites. Their stories may give us some direction as we try to balance family with leadership responsibilities. There is not time to extensively review every father/son combination in the history of the kings. We will briefly observe a few with an eye on something that may be beneficial to us as leader/parents.

> "More than a luxurious dwelling for royalty, a palace was designed to impress the king's subjects and foreign potentates. It was also a governmental and diplomatic center where the king met with his advisers, entertained supporters and visiting dignitaries in the great banquet hall, and dispensed justice."
>
> Jill Maynard, ed., *Bible Life and Times* (Pleasantville, NY: Reader's Digest Association, 1997), p. 261.

Absalom grew up in the house of David. Rehoboam grew up with the wisdom teaching of his dad Solomon. Jehoshaphat had a son named Jehoram who grew up throne-side. Ahaz became king after his father Jotham. Manasseh inherited the reign following Hezekiah. And Josiah's son Jehoahaz continued in the family business of the monarchy. All of these are father/son combinations who sat on the throne to lead God's people. And they all have something in common. The dads were leaders for God and the sons rebelled against Him.

We all know the description that best suited David. He was a man after God's own heart. As leaders, this both impresses us and inspires us as we strive for that ultimate compliment. We will talk later of the legacy that the leader David left for his people and future generations of kingly leadership. However, if there was a fatal leadership flaw in David, it was his inability to pass this passion for God on to his sons.

> "This book is lovingly dedicated to my dad, Charles Stanley, on whose shoulders I have been privileged to stand. It was from that vantage point that I caught a glimpse of what could be and should be for my life."
> Andy Stanley, *Visioneering* (Sisters, OR: Multnomah, 1999), p. 6.

David was in tune with the emotions of God. He knew what made God angry and what made Him smile. He sensed the things in man that pleased God and the issues that were important to Him. He knew God's word was right, and he spent time meditating on it. In a word David worshiped. He poured all of himself into every day with an awareness that God was with him, watching and guiding. Many times, these feelings were expressed in songs as he led the people in worship. But for some reason Absalom chose not to follow his father's example.

Absalom was David's third son, by his wife Maacah. He was raised by a man whose heart was after God's, but unfortunately Absalom did not inherit David's spiritual condition. Absalom was vengeful. He killed his half brother Amnon at a family reunion after holding a two-year grudge. He was concerned with his appearance. Scripture tells us that he had long, good-looking hair that he cut every year and weighed. He was also greedy and hungry for power—so much so that he tried to murder his father and steal his throne. There is no evidence that

> The local barber weighed the hair of Absalom's annual haircut and found it to be 200 shekels according to the royal standard. That's about five pounds of hair. (See 2 Samuel 14:26.)

he ever captured the same passion for God that his father did.

This result makes one wonder if David ever took the time to teach Absalom how to worship. It is the leader's job to nurture his family in worship of God. Many times church leaders work hard to develop a heart that beats with God, but they sometimes find it difficult to open up and share that journey with their children. Ideally, every church leader has an emotional love relationship with God. But is there any evidence of this to his children? Do they see this passion for His Name, His causes, and His church in the life that he displays for them at home? Do they worship side by side? Have they ever seen their father weep before God, cry out to Him, or praise Him with thanksgiving? We know David did all of these things, and yet Absalom somehow missed it.

In a similar story, Solomon eventually took his father's place of leadership. He staked his entire leadership strategy on wisdom as we have already discussed. He chose wisdom early. He began with wisdom, and good decisions marked his reign. Why then, did his son and successor Rehoboam make one of the worst decisions ever? Where were the years of experience and wisdom in this young man as he took over the leadership of a nation? How did Reho-

> Rehoboam's name means "enlarger of the people."

boam grow up in the house of the wisest man ever and end up so stupid?

It happened on the first day of his seventeen year reign. The oil from the coronation ceremony was still fresh in his beard. His father's advisors and boyhood friends shared the victory platform. Then the people began to chant for lower taxes. His father Solomon was wise, but his projects cost a lot of money and he had burdened the people with these expenses. This was campaign decision number one and he wisely sought advice.

The older, experienced counselors from his father's court recommended appeasement. "Tell them you'll relieve their burden." His younger friends (possibly drunk on the celebration wine and definitely intoxicated with their newfound power) advised a threat. "Dad was easy. I have more power in my pinkie than Dad had." Wisdom was shouting to listen to the older and wiser counsel, but Rehoboam turned from his father's pattern and made a decision that split the kingdom in two from that day forward. He facilitated Judah's spiritual decline into idol worship and collected wives and concubines like his dad. But he didn't display any leadership wisdom during the remainder of his life.

Solomon asked God to guide him in matters of leadership and judgment. He knew that every smart saying that ever came out of his mouth was directly from God. But either Rehoboam wasn't paying attention or he never sought the source of his father's wisdom. Or perhaps, Solomon became so distracted that he neglected sharing this important information with his son.

The leader's house can be full of teachable moments in which a demonstration of God's wisdom directs the decisions. Children will learn to seek God when the parents intentionally demonstrate that He is the source for all of their decision making. It must be noted that it is possible that Solomon tried to teach, but Rehoboam didn't pay attention. Children don't always follow the sound teaching and example of their parents. Perhaps Rehoboam thought that he could make decisions as wise as his father without God's help. Instead of seeking wisdom, he thought he could trust his own—making him as foolish as his father was smart.

Jehoshaphat was a great leader of the southern kingdom of Judah. He brought back some of the glory God's people had enjoyed under Solomon. He initiated a move to destroy all idol worship among his people. He also trained and sent Levites into the towns as a kind of traveling seminary to help educate people in God's ways. He was a good

> Amariah was the chief priest during the reign of Jehoshaphat and was put in charge of "any matter concerning the Lord." (See 2 Chronicles 19:11.)

king. However, when his son Jehoram followed, he rebuilt many of the altars and monuments to false gods that his father had managed to wipe out.

Jotham and Asa were much the same. The godly, leader-king Jotham spent his entire time in power leading the people back to God. He even repaired one of the temple gates to its original beauty. He

Follow God's Thread

God still had Levites who were interested in carrying out the spiritual duties of their ancestor Aaron.

spent a lifetime encouraging the worship of Jehovah and destroying idols. Then his son Asa took charge. He reinstated every idol and temple rite that his father had removed. He went so far as to sacrifice one of his sons to a false god!

These two examples show father/son combinations that exerted a lot of effort for opposite causes. I wonder if Jehoram or Asa were ever allowed to participate in the work their fathers led. It is important that the leader's family be involved in the work he is devoted to. Many pastors and church leaders have taken their families on international ministry trips or work trips. I believe this allows the child to witness God's work and purpose in the lives of his/her parents. The result is a deepened sense of ownership in the ministry from the kid's perspective. You can talk about the third world all you want, but when your children see it, they are forever affected. You can tell your kids stories of kingdom work, but experiencing the results firsthand leaves much more of an impression. If only Jehoram and Asa had helped their fathers chop down some Asherah poles, maybe it would have been harder to rebuild them later.

Finally, we come to Hezekiah and Manasseh. Hezekiah was a godly king who enjoyed success because of his faithfulness to God. Beyond that, he had a miraculous healing from a serious illness that a prophet had foretold would be fatal. In an act of mercy, God added fifteen years to this leader's life and Hezekiah served him faithfully to the end. Why then was his son so rebellious? He became one of Israel's most wicked kings, and he reigned longer than any other king over God's people. Even though God had moved miraculously in his father's life, Manasseh rejected His Lordship.

> The sign for Hezekiah's healing was one of two occasions in Scripture where time stopped or moved backwards. Hezekiah requested that the shadow go back ten steps on the stairway of Ahaz. (See 2 Kings 20:11 and Joshua 10:14.)

A closer examination of Scripture may suggest an answer for us in this situation. Manasseh was thirteen when he came to the throne. Have you done the math? This means that Hezekiah was healed two years before Manasseh was born. By the time, he was old enough to talk and understand, seven years had passed. Could it be that Hezekiah had neglected to share the story of how God added fifteen years to his life? How else could Manasseh have missed it?

> "The leader is a symbol as well as a 'keeper of the stories' concerning what God has been doing in that organization."
> Henry and Richard Blackaby, *Spiritual Leadership* (Nashville: Broadman and Holman, 2001), p. 80.

The great leader will make it a priority to tell and retell the stories of God's work in his life. Leadership homes should be oral history libraries of how God has been faithful over and over again. This increases the likelihood that the children of leaders will grow up knowing that God moves in the lives of His people; and they too will be inspired to desire relationship with this living God. Do your kids know of your conversion experience? What about your most recent spiritual victories? Can they recount miracle stories from your past?

What did you observe from these brief overviews of kings and princes? Did you notice some leadership implications for our ministries? Our kids are more likely to follow in our footsteps if we *teach them to worship.* How dif-

> "Impress them upon your children. Talk about them when you sit at home and when you walk along the road, when you lie down and when you get up" (Deuteronomy 6:7).

ferent Absalom may have been if David had worshiped with his son. Life in the palace should reflect a dependence *on God for the source of wisdom.* What decision might Rehoboam have made if his father taught him to seek God for wisdom? The leader's family should *be involved in the ministry of the leader.* If only Jehoram and Asa had been able to work side by side in ministry with their fathers, perhaps they wouldn't have become idolaters. Finally, leaders should frequently *recall godly victories.* Maybe Hezekiah's excited retelling of how God miraculously healed him would have encouraged Manasseh to trust in God.

There are two cautions as we observe these father/son rulers. The first is that a successful leader isn't a failure if his son or daughter doesn't follow in his leadership shoes. I think many of us place unfair expectations that our kids will grow up to be like us. This is probably true for firemen, doctors, and garbage men as well. Many parents secretly hope their children will respect their work enough to want to do the same thing.

The desire for your child to be what you are is unfair in any situation, but especially so for a calling as high as church leadership. A leader has to recognize the fact that, for whatever reason, God may not gift all (or any for that matter) of your children to lead like you do. We shouldn't worry that our kids grow up to be leaders in the church like us; we should pray that they come into relationship with Jesus like us. That's what really matters. You are not a bad leader if your children don't become pastors or missionaries, but you are if they end up faithless because of your neglect in their spiritual development.

The second caution is that sometimes children don't respond to godly parenting. Parenting is not a science, it's a journey; and we don't have all the details of these kings' journeys. We can see dimly as we read between the lines, but some of the kings mentioned above may have been good parents. Some church leaders parent well (by that I mean that they do their best to nurture their children in faith) and still end up with children who are far from God. This is sometimes hard to explain, but remember, we have the ability to continue to petition our children's creator—which is no small thing.

The challenge is to sit on the throne of leadership while continually nurturing the faith of those running around the palace. A leader who is sold out for the cause of Christ and dedicated to selling his family on that cause—in words, actions, and attitudes—will cause his children in the long run to enjoy the palace life.

CHAPTER TEN

Caring for Those You Lead

"Now the men of Israel were in distress that day, because Saul had bound the people under an oath, saying, 'Cursed be any man who eats food before evening comes, before I have avenged myself on my enemies!' So none of the troops tasted food" (1 Samuel 14:24).

"Then one of the soldiers told him, 'Your father bound the army under a strict oath, saying, 'Cursed be any man who eats food today!' That is why the men are faint. Jonathan said, 'My father has made trouble for the country. See how my eyes brightened when I tasted a little of this honey'" (1 Samuel 14:28-29).

"And for the whole army the victory was turned into mourning, because on that day the troops heard it said, 'The king is grieving for his son.' The men stole into the city that day as men steal in who are ashamed when they flee from battle" (2 Samuel 19:2-3).

"Now go out and encourage your men. I swear by the LORD that if you don't go out, not a man will be left with you by nightfall. . . . So the king got up and took his seat in the gateway. When the men were told, 'The king is sitting in the gateway,' they all came before him" (2 Samuel 19:7-8).

Those who follow have needs. Leaders sometimes miss this because they are busy fighting for causes, launching new ideas, dreaming new visions, and planning for what's next. But a great leader understands why people follow. People follow because they believe the leader can take them somewhere they couldn't go on their own.

"Most people will do nearly anything for you if you treat them respectfully. And that means making it clear to them that their feelings are important, their preferences are respected, and their opinions are valuable."

John C. Maxwell and Jim Donnan, *Becoming a Person of Influence* (Nashville: Thomas Nelson, 1997), p. 114.

And they are not only loyal because of the destination, but because they trust that the leader genuinely cares for them. People who willingly submit to leadership trust that the leader will take care of their physical and emotional needs. Faithful followers want and desire more than just winning victories. They hope to experience victories which affirm that their leaders truly care for them.

> "Workers have social needs at work. They want the ability to plan their workday with their co-workers and to communicate briefly throughout the day about progress and problems."
>
> Dennis A. Romig, Ph.D., *Side-by-Side Leadership* (Atlanta: Bard Press, 2001), p. 37.

Saul was at war with the Philistines . . . again. He was so close to victory against his pagan enemies, he could taste it. As a matter of fact, his intense hunger to defeat them satisfied his appetite more than food. So he made a rash decision. This was a typical move for Saul. By his decree neither he nor his men, on pain of death, would eat anything until they were victorious and had pushed the opposition out of their land. He made this perfectly clear to everyone from his generals on down. "No food until we win!"

> The Philistines were inhabitants of Canaan before Abraham. They appear in his story as a tribe of people who lived near Gerar. (See Genesis 26:1.)

Meanwhile, his son Jonathan had taken his armor-bearer to stir things up at the Philistine outpost. The king's son taunted the enemy as he walked through a valley where they occupied the cliffs. He told his armor-bearer, "Let's go pick a fight and see if God helps us win a battle." They asked God to guide them by the answer the Philistines would give. If the Philistines told Jonathan and his armor-bearer to wait in the valley while the Philistines made their way down the cliffs, God was telling them to run. But if their enemies encouraged them to come up the side of the bluff to fight, then God was giving the Philistines into their hands. The Philistines challenged Jonathan and his assistant to come on up. So they did, and, by the hand of God, they killed twenty Philistines.

This set off a chain of events that brought victory for Israel. The tag team warfare of Jonathan and his servant caused a panic to strike the Philistine army. They began killing each other. God sent an earthquake, and they fled. Noticing what was happening: Saul blew the trumpet for war and men from all over Israel pursued and plundered. They chased them for hours, fighting valiantly, but the Scripture says they were distressed.

Every man in Saul's army was distressed because they were hungry. You can't assemble that many men together and call them to physical activity without the promise of nourishment. Just try getting people to help you move by saying, "Today we are going to focus on the move. No one eats until every box and piece of furniture is moved." You'll have trouble getting volunteers. Conversely, men will lift heavy furniture all day long if there's some free pizza in it for them. The usual custom in moving is to feed the movers.

> "Any valuable possessions were considered plunder, including livestock, clothing, jewelry, women, and children. According to the concept of holy war explained in Deuteronomy 20, God allowed the plundering of cities outside the Holy Land."
>
> Jill Maynard, ed., *Bible Life and Times* (Pleasantville, NY: Reader's Digest Association, 1997), p. 277.

In the same way, in the days of the kings part of the reward for the men who fought the battle was that they were allowed to eat some of the plunder. In this instance, the men were winning the battle, but they weren't having any fun. The only thing they could think about was how hungry they were.

There was, however, one fighter who looked refreshed as he chased the Philistine army that day. That man was Jonathan. He was strengthened because as he ran through the woods, hot on the trail of the enemy, he came across some honey. The men saw it, but kept going. Jonathan saw it and took a coffee break. He hadn't heard the decree of his father, and

> "Beekeeping was probably not practiced in Palestine before the fourth century BC, when hives were made of wicker and straw" (Ibid., p. 177).

so he ate and was strengthened for battle. When one of the men told him of his father's decree he lamented that his father had made such a leadership mistake.

Finally, after the men had expelled the enemy army, they were so exhausted (fatigued from lack of food) that nearly every one of them pounced on the nearest animal, slaughtered it, and began eating it raw. Of course, this was against Jewish law, but they were so famished because of Saul's hasty oath, they ignored the rules. Saul had to set up a makeshift butcher shop to keep them from sinning.

They won the victory that day, but something just wasn't right about the celebration.

Follow God's Thread

Even though Saul was not at his best, God turned the tide of the entire battle for Saul and his men when the Philistines became afraid. It was "a panic sent by God." (See 1 Samuel 14:15.)

Another battle is recorded for us in the stories of the kings that lends itself to our discussion on caring for those you lead. We have already mentioned this story in chapter seven, but there is more. David's army had overcome Absalom's rebellion, but again the victory celebration was strange.

During the battle, a young man had come upon Absalom. He was caught by his hair, hanging defenseless from a tree. In fear, this young warrior refused to kill the rebel prince, but Joab, David's commander, rode onto the scene and ran Absalom through with three javelins. He immediately blew the trumpet calling off David's troops and rallying them home to celebrate the victory, but by the time the men had returned to the town where the king was staying, word had gotten to them that the king was mourning his son's death. When they got closer, they heard their leader's weeping and wailing for themselves.

There was not one, "Good job, guys!" They didn't hear their leader thank them for saving his life and the lives of his family. No one felt a familiar congratulatory pat on the back for all his hard work. Instead, they snuck into town quietly and told of the day's happenings in hushed tones. All the while, David continued in his depressed state. By the time Joab had returned from the battle-field, he thought he was in the wrong place. Where was the party?

Something came over Joab in that moment. Perhaps he recalled how nervous they had all been that morning before heading into battle. He might have remembered the adrenaline rush of fear and excitement evident in his warriors' eyes. Maybe, it was a deep understanding of the sacrifice these men had made. It might just have been a leadership moment for Joab. Whatever the reason, it was only a matter of

"One of the best parts . . . of any leadership role is getting the chance to let people know how much their work means to you."
Rudolph Giuliani, *Leadership* (New York: Miramax Books, 2002), p. 40.

minutes before Joab stood over the grieving king and rebuked him for reacting to victory in this way. He threatened that if David chose not to come out and encourage his men, they would all be gone—then and possibly for the rest of his reign.

David received this wise counsel, and he set his own loss aside. The king went to the gate of the city and took his seat in the presence of the people. When the warriors heard that their leader was waiting to see them, they all made their way to the gate as well. We assume that in this moment, King David spoke the words of encouragement that they all longed to hear.

Two different kings and two different victories: one big leadership lesson. It is important for a leader to recognize and meet the needs of his followers. Without this consideration, followers might quickly resemble the exhausted and discouraged men of these two armies. In the end, you'll either have an ineffective team or risk losing your team entirely. These two stories illustrate how a leader must pay attention to both the physical and emotional needs of his people.

With the privilege of church leadership comes responsibility. The only way a leader can expect effective ministry from both volunteers and paid staff is to demonstrate to them that they are cared for and appreciated. Saul's men were more than willing to fight for his cause, but they also wanted the assurance that, come supper time, there would be something to eat. David's men gladly fought for their leader, but they needed some encouragement for a job well done.

Volunteers hold the church together. By God's design, the individual gifts of those who are part of the church get the job done when it comes to kingdom work. Leaders are called to coordinate these gifts by equipping and inspiring them for the cause. Many times, however, church leaders are strong on inspiring but short on equipping and encouraging.

> "Now to each one a manifestation of the Spirit is given for the common good" (1 Corinthians 12:7).

Volunteers expect us to supply them with the tools they need to get the job done. This can be anything from teaching materials such as workbooks and writing instruments to personal contact and support or providing the proper training necessary to get the job done. Sadly, many of the volunteers in our churches are in as much distress as Saul's men were because leaders are not feeding them the tools necessary to win the battle. Or like David's men, they don't feel encouraged as they make sacrifices for the cause of Christ.

Full-time, paid staff members have additional needs that church leaders are called to meet. Like their volunteer counterparts, they too flourish when they are given the right tools for the job. They become better ministers when they have access to a reasonable budget. Too many staff members get discouraged because they can't accomplish ministry goals for lack of funds. A leader also needs to pay attention to the proper equipment for ministry. Phone systems, computers, and functional office equipment make the job a little easier. The opportunity for continuing education through conferences, books, and postgraduate studies can also increase a team member's effectiveness.

An even deeper concern for today's church leader is the care for the personal finances of each staff member. Obviously, most people who are called to ministry are not in it for the money, but the good leader will see to it that they are paid a fair wage for the work they do. This is the right thing to do because of the biblical teaching about it, but it will also "brighten the eyes" of the minister who is compensated well. This means the good leader will pay attention to cost of living, retirement concerns, and business expenses on behalf of the staff. This allows your team to have peace at home and focus on ministry instead of monthly bills.

One final word about taking care of the physical needs of those who work for us: don't assume they want to sacrifice the way you do. Leaders have a deeper ownership of the vision, which means they should sacrifice more, give more, and overlook their own monetary concerns for the good of the organization. Saul wanted to win so badly, he was willing to give up food for the victory. His mistake was in assuming his men wanted to make the same sacrifice. Today's leader may often be willing to forgo raises, cut conference allowances, and give sacrificially to the building fund, but he shouldn't assume that his team members want to do the same.

This discussion about meeting the needs of the people who follow brings us to this question: "Is it enough to only take care of our team's physical needs?" More directly, "Will my volunteers and employees be satisfied and fully motivated if I give them the materials they need and pay them well?" The answer is "No." It is also necessary for today's leader to be an encourager. The word means "to give courage," and the tasks we call our followers to undertake require courage. It is discouraging to teach and not see immediate results. It is discouraging to plan a program that fails. It is discouraging to be part of a church that isn't growing or is struggling financially. It can be frustrating to sacrifice behind the scenes with absolutely no recognition. Sometimes church work can be as thankless as winning a war and then having your leader lament the fact that you won!

Finally, staff members who follow a church pastor or organization president, have a need to be fed in the deepest of ways. Most of them look to the leader for their spiritual needs to be met. They desire to work for someone who leads the way in devotional practices, prayer, and sensitivity to the Spirit's leading. The great leader regularly prays for and with his staff, pushes them to new personal growth, and guides them with spiritual wisdom. Staff members hunger for this spiritual care and the great leader will feed it.

The volunteers we work with need encouragement by the way that we recognize them. Appreciation banquets might be thought of as out of date, but even the simplest thank you can go a long way. Simple handwritten notes to thank volunteers is also an effective means of encouragement. Taking time in a worship service or meeting to note special volunteer accomplishments increases the team spirit in our lay people. Thanking individuals as we pass them "on the job" means more to them than we might think.

These are only a few examples of how a leader might spur his team on. The leader is called, like David, to "go out and encourage his men." This will increase follower productivity and their sense of fulfillment because they know their leader values them and notices their contributions to the team. It causes them to try harder and prepares them for the upcoming challenges. Yes, there would be more battles for King David's men to fight.

If it is important to monitor the encouragement level in volunteers, it is even more so for the paid staff. You may show staff appreciation in a number of ways. The leader should regularly observe his staff at work. Some may think this could make employees nervous to be watched by the "boss," but it actually presents an opportunity for demonstrating their effectiveness to their leader. It is a good idea to let them know in advance that you are there to support them and cheer them on in what they are doing for the cause.

A good leader will also meet with staff regularly to maintain a level of friendship and of sharing a life of ministry together. This goes beyond the official meetings that are commonplace. Staff members appreciate the casual drop-in visit that is focused on their personal growth, ministry, and family concerns. These impromptu meetings show that you care about them as individuals and are not just using them to accomplish your own goals. Be careful not to come with a hidden agenda or use these times to subtly reprimand them. Making a habit of these casual discussions will cause the follower to trust the leader more.

> "One leader I knew would go to each contributor's desk at least once a day, ostensibly to drop off some document or ask a question. Actually, he was creating an opportunity for each person to interact, perhaps to share an idea."
> Dennis Romig, Ph.D., *Side-by-Side Leadership* (Atlanta: Bard Press, 2001), p. 153.

Finally, staff members are encouraged when the leader notes their strengths and nurtures development in those specific areas. Sincere compliments that point out specific instances of success go a long way in encouraging your team. Phrases like, "You really are a gifted speaker" or "I see Jesus in you when you talk to people" cause people to focus even more intently on that which comes naturally. This makes them more effective pastors, and it makes you a more biblical leader.

> "But encourage one another daily, as long as it is called Today, so that none of you may be hardened by sin's deceitfulness" (Hebrews 3:13).

Followers have needs. When those needs are not met, followers can be distressed and ready to quit like the men of David and Saul. In great leadership moments we feed them and encourage them. When their spirits are refreshed, we will find them sitting with us at the gate awaiting the next challenge for God. Care for those who follow you, and they will find it easy to care for you.

CHAPTER ELEVEN
S × P = A

"Amaziah son of Joash king of Judah began to reign. . . . He did what was right in the eyes of the LORD. . ." (2 Kings 14:1,3).

"He was the one who defeated ten thousand Edomites in the Valley of Salt and captured Sela in battle, calling it Joktheel, the name it has to this day" (2 Kings 14:7).

"But Jehoash king of Israel replied to Amaziah king of Judah. . . . 'You have indeed defeated Edom and now you are arrogant. Glory in your victory, but stay at home! Why ask for trouble and cause your own downfall and that of Judah also?'" (2 Kings 14:9-10).

I t certainly is strange to begin a chapter from a leadership book with an abstract algebraic equation. But it's more than an author's attempt to find a use for the formulas learned in high school math. Actually, it will make sense if you understand the "S" as success and the "P" as power. In the leader's life, power multiplied by success often equals "A" or arrogance.

> "Pride closes leaders' minds. When leaders believe their own abilities are solely responsible for their organization's success, they dangerously assume no one else could run their organization as well as they can."
>
> Henry and Richard Blackaby, *Spiritual Leadership* (Nashville: Broadman and Holman, 2001), p. 233.

Wait just a minute. Didn't we discuss this issue in chapter one? Remember, we talked about Saul and his humility as he hid in the baggage at the coronation? Likewise, David didn't speak badly of the Lord's anointed or think himself worthy to marry the king's daughter. Haven't we already been here? Isn't this discussion on arrogance just a rehash of the same old subject?

Two comments: One, pride seems to be such a problem among today's leaders that another chapter on the topic couldn't hurt. Two, although

> "Pride goes before destruction, a haughty spirit before a fall" (Proverbs 16:18).

pride is obviously the opposite of humility, one is a state of mind we try to avoid, and the other is an attitude we work to attain. This means that a discussion about arrogance has to be more substantive than "the opposite of humility." If that were the case, battling arrogance would simply be a matter of remaining humble. Easier said than done.

> "All of you, clothe yourselves with humility toward one another, because, 'God opposes the proud but gives grace to the humble.' Humble yourselves, therefore, under God's mighty hand, that he may lift you up in due time" (1 Peter 5:5-6).

Staying humble is for most a major challenge. Humility is an attitude many leaders begin with as they realize the size of the calling they have responded to. It is true that some may begin with a prideful heart because they lack judgment. Sometimes ignorance breeds pride. But humility is something that most Christian leaders would say they desire. Why then does pride appear to be the common battleground for most leaders as they climb the proverbial ladder? Humility seems to come easy in the early stages when one isn't sure of one's leadership abilities, but pride seems to follow those who have even minimal success.

Saul began with an unassuming attitude but became prideful enough to offer the prebattle sacrifice without the prophet. David began with a heart that beat "unworthy," but spending time on the throne brought about an arrogance that allowed him to steal another man's wife. Many of today's leaders start with the most sincere and humble of motives but they end up with a leadership style that communicates superiority to all those around them.

Chapter one was an encouragement to stay humble. This chapter is about confronting pride as a leadership issue. There is one more interesting contrast that deserves mentioning before we go on. David and Solomon had arrogant moments because of their title and authority (kingship as well as church leadership has its privileges). But the king we will examine in this instance became prideful, not because he was a ruler, but because he was successful.

Amaziah was twenty-five years old when some palace officials plotted to kill his father. The rest area in Beth Millo on a road trip to Silla was the location of the murder of Joash. History doesn't record why he was assassinated or why the assassins would allow his son to succeed him, but this is the somewhat tragic way Amaziah became king. He continued many of the religious reforms that his father had begun. Both were good kings although they didn't fully wipe out idol worship.

> Beth Millo literally means "the house of the mound."

After some time on the throne, Amaziah took notice that the people who had plotted against his father still held positions in the palace court. Through strong leadership, he had earned the respect of his people and so, to avenge his father, he had the murderers put to death. This established his authority throughout his kingdom as a just but fair king. He spared the lives of the sons of these murderers in accordance with Jewish law.

With his palace and power then intact, he turned his attention to an old enemy of Judah, the Edomites. The country of Edom lay to the south and east of Jerusalem where these descendants of Esau lived sometimes in subjection to, sometimes in freedom from, and many times in war against the Israelites. On this occasion, Amaziah led his troops to battle in the Valley of Salt in which the Dead Sea is located.

> Salt was abundant from the mines near the Dead Sea and was apparently used as a part of certain Jewish sacrifices. (See Leviticus 2:13.)

It must have been an incredible place for a fight. Crystallized salt formations served as bunkers and obstacles as these two armies battled. Again, Amaziah showed great leadership in guiding his troops to victory. History records that he killed ten thousand Edomites in that battle. As a result one of their most important cities was taken and renamed Joktheel.

The long ride north was a triumphant march. No doubt every town hosted a victory parade with Amaziah as the hero and center of attention. "Amazing Amaziah" became the chant, and his reputation as a great king and leader was sealed. He returned to the Jerusalem palace physically tired but emotionally energized. After a royal bath and a late night snack, he lay in his king-size bed (what did you expect?) and wondered what he would do next.

The next morning he must have been feeling confident as he enjoyed breakfast with a view of the city. "Dear Jehoash," he dictated to a scribe, "I, the king of Judah, challenge you to a battle. Winner take all." A messenger flew north with the message. Since the time of Jeroboam and Rehoboam, the two kingdoms (Israel in the north and Judah in the south) had divided God's people into two separate nations. Over the years, they had co-existed, mostly peacefully, but now Amaziah was going to challenge his Israelite brothers, specifically their king, Jehoash.

At this time, the Israelites outnumbered the people of Judah. They had more territory and a bigger army. Judah was comprised of basically two tribes, while the other ten tribes made up Israel. The king of Israel had read in the *Monthly King Gazette*

> At the division of the two kingdoms, we learn that Judah remained loyal to David's descendants, but later when Rehoboam mustered an army, the tribe of Benjamin was also numbered with Judah. (See 1 Kings 12:20-21.)

that his southern brother had beaten back the Edomite army. But he didn't expect to be the next target. He sent a reply to Amaziah that basically communicated to this aggressive king how impossible it would be to defeat his army. He encouraged him to enjoy the victory over Edom but to leave Israel alone.

Follow God's Thread

Jehoash was by no means a godly king, yet he gave Amaziah wise advice concerning his arrogance. Amazingly, God spoke through this wicked king a warning about arrogance that still rings true for leaders today.

Amaziah wasn't taking advice. Everything he had done up to this point had been successful. He convinced his people, his palace servants, his advisors, and his army that they would again be victorious. Unfortunately, this was not the voice of wisdom; it was pride. He had so much pride that he brought some of the Edomite gods into his palace. Then he threatened one of Jehovah's prophets and rejected God's warning not to fight against Israel. Even the ungodly king he had challenged identified this arrogant attitude. But since Amaziah wanted war, he got it.

In the city of Beth Shemesh, Amaziah's army was routed and the men fled to their homes. As the army dwindled, the king was

> Beth Shemesh was established by Joshua as one of the towns that would make up the northern border of Judah. (See Joshua 15:10.)

captured and taken back to his capital city. He watched in chains as Jehoash had his men destroy a large section (two football fields in length) of Jerusalem's wall. They also looted the temple, taking everything of value in it. They took valuables from the palace, and they carried off hostages. As they made their way out of town, they released this once proud king.

Amaziah limped through the rubble into the throne room. As the dust settled, he could see they had taken all the weapons and artifacts that his fathers had collected. The walls were cold and bare. The palace, the city, the kingdom, and the temple were only shells of their former selves. The cries and mourning of the people filled the streets. Where there had once been the sounds of victory and music, there was silence and despair. The great leader Amaziah had become prideful, and the price he paid for it was high.

Things didn't get better for Amaziah. Unfortunately, a plot not unlike the one that took his father's life was carried out against him. He was assassinated and replaced as leader. This once powerful leader for God died at the hands of those who had loyally followed him into battle. Of course, most church leaders don't face assassination attempts by their leadership board, but the example of Amaziah still speaks to today's leader.

Arrogance is a progression from humble trust and dependence on God to reliance and security in self and other gods. This shift in dependence is always an equation that ends with ineffective leadership even though it often begins with great potential. Amaziah's arrogance may have begun when he successfully avenged his father. The subtle attitude of superiority may have formed in his heart while the crowds cheered him home from the Edom victory. This teaches us that leaders must pay close attention to their emotions when they experience great leadership moments.

Let's face it, for a godly leader there is nothing more exhilarating than spiritual success. When the preacher nails a sermon, it is intoxicating. When a Christian administrator seals a financial deal that brings monetary gain to the organization, it is thrilling. When a long-planned, extensive church program exceeds everyone's expectations, the leader is satisfied. When the new staff hire excels, the leader takes pride in his ability to evaluate personalities. Success in ministry is a great feeling, but it can also be very dangerous for the soul.

The good leader must take an honest emotional inventory every time he senses victory. Of course, the Sunday school response is, "We couldn't have done this without God." This is true, but can easily be spoken while a voice in the heart whispers, "God couldn't have done it without me." When the giving

> "No, I beat my body and make it my slave so that after I have preached to others, I myself will not be disqualified for the prize" (1 Corinthians 9:27).

exceeds the budget, the capital campaign reaches its goal, and the attendance continues to increase, the church leader must force himself to answer a critical question: "Who gets credit for this?" Leaders who constantly remind themselves that it is God's power bringing the victory will be less likely to slip into arrogance.

The telltale signs of embryonic arrogance are found in the simple words "I," "my," and "mine." A person who refers to a work as "my church," says, "I led this or that campaign," or admits "the authority is mine" is dancing dangerously close to arrogance. This is true even if the words come while talking to yourself. For Amaziah, it was "my army" that "I led" and "the victory is mine." Any leader who uses this kind of language is verbalizing personal ownership of the victory. It may be okay for the leader to acknowledge his participation, but God owns every positive result in His kingdom.

On the heels of owning leadership success comes the belief that the victory was a result of "my power." This is a ludicrous idea. No right-minded Christian leader would claim to have extraordinary power, but this is the natural progression of our fallen nature. The moment the leader claims the victory is his, he will soon believe it is not only his, but it's

> "This is the word of the Lord to Zerubbabel: 'Not by might nor by power, but by my Spirit,' says the LORD Almighty" (Zechariah 4:6).

because he is so good. This is a crucial step towards arrogance because it begins to eliminate God from the equation. Perhaps this is why Amaziah brought the false gods home. If indeed it was his ability that brought the victory, then any old god would do. He did not feel a need for God's guidance in his leadership direction.

The process of self trust leads to an ever increasing state of arrogance. When God's leader no longer seeks God's direction, God's will is often left unsought as well. Remember, above all, that we are leading an eternal kingdom that God has planned, executed, and orchestrated. Israel was not a kingdom for Amaziah to conquer. God had a plan for His people of the northern kingdom. In the same way, our position of church leadership is not for our gain. God's motives move us in the right direction, while the motives of man tend to lean towards selfishness and destruction.

Why did Amaziah want to attack Israel? Was it God's plan to reunite the kingdom? Apparently, Amaziah wasn't asking. He was motivated by his own pride to add to his list of accomplishments. The warriors of Judah who died in battle that day needlessly lost their lives for the greed of a tyrant. Don't call people to sacrifice for anything other than the will of God. Influencing people to build, serve, risk, and pray for our personal goals is the highest form of leadership abuse. It is true arrogance.

The end of leadership arrogance is defeat. Ironically, as victory sometimes leads to pride, pride leads to defeat. The very opposite of the victory that grew into pride is the tragic end for the leader who isn't humble. Many initially successful church leaders have become warped, tyrannical bosses who misuse their authority for personal gain. Sadly, they lose credibility and the ability to influence the people of God for His purposes. In the end, they are only shells of their former ministry selves as they survey the devastation of battles fought without the Lord's help.

We can combat this attitude of pride by doing exactly the opposite of what Amaziah did. As leaders we avoid arrogance by celebrating God's victory, acknowledging our weaknesses, and remembering God's lordship.

We celebrate God's victories by daily recounting how God has worked miraculously in our personal lives and in the work He has called us to. We can practice this by telling someone who is close to us how God deserves credit for recent victories. To do this, simply list events, people who have grown or changed, or results that you consider successes. By each of these victories write a brief description of how God did it. Tell someone.

Confession is good for the soul they say, and it is also a great way to stay humble. We sometimes have trouble admitting our weaknesses, sins, and inabilities. Again, making a list of sins we've committed, abilities we don't have, and areas in which we are weak can be beneficial. This is time for honesty. Every time we succeed in leadership, we pull that list out and thank God that we could be a part of something so grand.

To remember that lordship belongs to God, we can create visual reminders to give us kingdom perspective. On the wall of my office I have an old church attendance board. The statistics are those of April 12, 1964, a little under a year before I was born. Often, I look at that board and am reminded that before I was born, God was doing a work at the church I serve. It is my visual reminder that this is God's deal, not mine. This compels me to think in terms of His kingdom work. We may use touching pictures, famous sayings, favorite Scripture verses, or some religious artifacts that remind us of God's ownership of the ministry to which he has called us. Hopefully, these reminders will keep us from taking charge of what belongs to Him and keep us humble.

What might Amaziah have written in his journal the night of the victorious battle? What would he have written if he kept God's power in perspective?

Amaziah's Journal, April 12, 702 B.C.

> Today's victory was amazing. When I saw the charging army of Edom advancing against our troops, I was scared . . . so I prayed. "God, you told me to come down here to the Valley of Salt and fight your battle. Since it's your battle, I need your strength. I can't do it. I'm not a very good shot with the bow, and I can't keep a chariot on the road. But the men of Judah are following me. Grant us success today by your will and for your glory. Amen." By the time I had finished praying, the horn sounded for battle and the charge was on. Miraculously, God destroyed our enemies before us. One of my generals told me we had killed ten thousand Edomites. It seemed like more to me. I'm tired, but I feel good. God gave us victory today. I will trust His will for my place in His kingdom until my dying day.

What if Amaziah had lived out these words of humility? What if you and I did?

CHAPTER TWELVE
View to a Temptation

"David sent Joab out with the king's men and the whole Israelite army. They destroyed the Ammonites and besieged Rabbah. But David remained in Jerusalem. One evening David got up from his bed and walked around on the roof of the palace. From the roof he saw a woman bathing. The woman was very beautiful, and David sent someone to find out about her" (2 Samuel 11:1-3).

A dultery. Theft. Rape. Murder. These are not comfortable words. These are not Christian words. These words do not describe actions that most "morally good" people would consider acceptable. In the church, they cover at least three of the Ten Big Ones that have been no-no's since God's conversation with Moses on a desert mountain. They certainly aren't words associated with church leaders. Yet the greatest of God's Old Testament kings was guilty of all of these.

> "The time to buy the smoke alarm is when you build the house, not after the fire starts. The time to enlist friends as partners in accountability is not when sexual temptation is already a raging inferno but before the first spark."
>
> Henry and Richard Blackaby, *Spiritual Leadership* (Nashville: Broadman and Holman, 2001), p. 238.

Even if this chapter hadn't begun with the Scripture about David and Bathsheba you would have figured it out. Next to Peter's denial of Jesus on the night of his betrayal, this may be the most famous failure in the Bible. We as leaders are strangely attracted to this story and its

> "You shall not murder. You shall not commit adultery. You shall not steal" (Exodus 20:13-15).

epilogue, Psalm 51. We are drawn to the failure of a man so close to God's heart because we hope to see ourselves there. We too are

leaders who have failed morally and have uttered our own peni-
tent pleas.

Before we proceed any further on this chapter about temptations, let me apologize to any woman leader for a chapter that
focuses even more on an issue that is directed towards male leadership. It's true that most men struggle with the "view" thing.
God has wired us to be visual when it comes to sexuality and so
we are tempted sexually by sight. However, women are still vulnerable to Satan's schemes. The temptations may present themselves in different ways, but just as many women commit adultery
as men (funny how adultery usually involves two parties). If you
are a woman who leads, read on, the lessons learned will be just as
valuable to you.

Some of you who are reading this sentence are struggling
with pornography even as you read. Some of you are so guilt-rid-
den that you skipped to this
chapter to see if there are any
new words of hope for a leader
who struggles in the area of sexual temptation. Still others have
physically committed adultery,
and you wonder if you can possibly go on acting like a leader

> "What makes pornography so addictive
> is that more than anything else in a lost
> man's life, it makes him feel like a man
> without ever requiring a thing of him."
> John Eldredge, *Wild at Heart* (Nash-
> ville: Thomas Nelson, 2001), p. 44.

when you feel like a lawbreaker. Finally, many of you read with a
sense of sadness as you recall how many of your ministry friends
have fallen prey to this evil trap. Though this story is 3,000 years
old, it is more relevant than it has ever been.

David was a man of war, and it was war season. This
Scripture announces spring as the time for war just like one would
say it's baseball season or football season or time for school to
begin. Apparently, kings got spring fever every year for a good
old-fashioned battle. If they didn't have an enemy, they'd go pick
a fight with someone. It was time to get out the old sword and
polish it up (or better yet, have some smith forge a new one). It
was time to get back into shape so that you could fit into your
armor. Springtime for a king was time to get the troops together
and recall victories from years gone by and lay out strategies for
the coming season. It was time for war and David was a man of
war, but David stayed home.

Why did David stay home? Was he getting old and tired and just didn't physically feel like heading into battle? Maybe he had slain so many thousands that it just wasn't fun cutting down opponents any more. Perhaps the king was content with what he already had in his palace in Jerusalem. War may have just become so routine for him that he was looking for something different. This is not the point of the story, but it is worth mentioning, for if David had gone to war as usual, perhaps he wouldn't have earned this black mark on his otherwise stellar record. But David sent his army out under the command of Joab while he stayed home.

While the men were at war, David suffered from insomnia. Apparently David couldn't sleep one night, so he threw on his house robe and sandals and walked out onto the terrace to take in the fresh, spring night air. Imagine a penthouse suite with a view. From this vantage point he could see the lights flickering in the temple courtyard. On the other end of the porch, he could peer into the eerie darkness of the Kidron valley. Oil lamps illuminated house after house. The king had quite a view from his palace. Perhaps the view was too good, and it wasn't long before he saw her.

> "The earliest lamps were stone bowls filled with melted animal fat, in which floated a wick of twisted plant fibers. These were replaced by pottery bowls, the lamps mentioned in the Bible. The principal fuel for these lamps was olive oil."
>
> Jill Maynard, ed., *Bible Life and Times* (Pleasantville, NY: Readers' Digest Association, 1997), p. 206.

Bathsheba was taking a bath. Many wise men and scholars have argued about whether she was enticing David or simply trying to get clean. The Scripture doesn't really place any blame on her, so it would seem that she was unaware that someone was watching. David quickly summoned a servant and asked about who this beautiful woman was. By his command she was standing in the presence of the king within the hour.

It was lust that brought this woman into the bedroom of the king. Many have wondered why she gave in so willingly, but to focus on this issue is to miss the point. David saw a beautiful woman and then acted upon the lust that this vision stirred in his heart. This was not love. He selfishly used her for a short time of passion and then sent her home. We don't know if he had plans to ever see her again. He had given in to sexual temptation, but this sin had only begun to do its damage. There are always consequences!

It wasn't long before news came from Bathsheba announcing she was pregnant with the king's child. This revelation set off a whirlwind of scheming on David's part. First he thought of bringing Uriah home from the front lines and giving him some R & R. David's hope was that Uriah would sleep with his wife and be fooled into thinking the child was his own. However, this loyal soldier refused to enjoy home life while the other men in the army were still on the battlefield. So Uriah refused to go home. He slept in the courtyard with the king's servants.

> Uriah was a part of an elite force known as David's mighty men. This group of thirty men were David's best warriors. (See 2 Samuel 23:39.)

Still scheming, David invited Uriah to dine with him the next evening. He deliberately got this faithful warrior drunk in hopes he would stagger home to his wife. No luck. Again, he slept on a mat in the courtyard. This prompted David to sink to his lowest level of deceit. He prepared a note instructing Joab to expose Uriah to a battle position which would assure his death at the hands of the enemy. Joab was called upon to carry out Uriah's death sentence sealed with the king's royal stamp.

David anxiously waited for a report from the front lines. Before long, the expected news arrived. Uriah was dead. Sadly, David had conspired against one of his mighty men—a group of thirty-three of Israel's special forces. David's wicked coverup now allowed him to bring Bathsheba into the palace as his own wife. David was convinced no one would ever know.

It might have been the end of the story if God hadn't spoken through a prophet named Nathan. God told him to confront king David about his sin. Cleverly, the prophet told a parable to illustrate the seriousness of David's sin and enticed David into wording his own condemnation: "Whoever did this deserves to die!"

> Nathan first appears in Scripture holding a conversation with David about building the temple. (See 2 Samuel 7:2-3.)

His leadership judgment wasn't dulled even as he lived in the sin of adultery. After Nathan's famous "You are the man" speech, David fell to the floor in conviction. Not long after, David penned the famous song of repentance known to us as Psalm 51. All of this because of a view from the palace porch.

What lessons can today's leader learn from this king's experience? Stay off the porch. Go to war. Don't look. When you see a woman bathing, walk away. All sound advice. They may seem too simplistic, but there are great lessons to be learned here.

First, every leader needs to know that temptations will come his way. The Bible teaches very clearly that Satan is a scheming, lying, light-simulating, arrow-shooting, loud-mouthed lion. And he is intent on destroying leaders. There is a possibility that he timed the bath with the insomnia. He may have moved Bathsheba into the light and David to that end of the porch. He could have influenced David to

> "And no wonder, for Satan himself masquerades as an angel of light" (1 Corinthians 11:13).

stay at home while nudging Uriah to enlist for battle. Attention, leader. Be on your guard. The evil snake that was bold enough to tempt the Son of God will definitely slither into your life.

But just being on guard against temptation won't keep us from falling. It is important to identify our weaknesses. There are temptations that are individually specific. Because of our past, some are prone to drink too much. Some are given to laziness. Certain individuals struggle with gambling. This is time for ruthless honesty. There comes a time when we all must look in the mirror and admit to ourselves and to God what our weaknesses are. Satan strikes at our weakness. Why do you think he asked Jesus to make bread? He knew the Savior had just completed a fast and was hungry. Jesus overcame this temptation because he knew Satan would strike at His human need for food. In the same way, identifying our individual weaknesses will give us an advantage in avoiding temptations.

Men, I didn't list lust in the examples above, but it had better be on your list. If it's not, you're not being honest with yourself. God created you to be stimulated by a woman's naked body. If he hadn't made us this way, Adam may have been disinterested in God's new creation when she appeared on the scene in the garden. Instead, God gave us this wonderful, dangerous gift of visual sexuality. A woman's body is alluring to a man. That's a part of God's design.

This design will bring harmony to your marriage if enjoyed with your wife. It will destroy both your ministry and marriage if it is abused. Leader for God, please be honest and admit that sexual temptation is an issue. Ignoring it or denying it will not keep us from being tempted. As we identify our weaknesses, we are able to battle temptation more effectively.

The leader must also battle temptation by noticing times when the struggle seems strong. David wasn't doing anything. He wasn't engaged in any positive activity for God. If he had been, he wouldn't have had time for Bathsheba. Many leaders fall into temptation in down times. When ministry activity slows down after a major campaign or particularly draining season, we can become vulnerable to temptation. When we aren't focused on leading for God, we sometimes drift from Him.

There are other times we should be on guard for temptation. When leaders get tired, we are susceptible to Satan's snares. In times when we find ourselves physically exhausted, we just want a break. In emotionally depleting times, we may be more vulnerable to a temptation that can give us an emotional high. This often comes in the form of wrong relationship. In spiritually weak times, our prayer is nonexistent, our time in the Word is sparse, and the Spirit's influence is dulled. There are two suggestions here for the leader on the topic of being overtired. 1) Don't let yourself get exhausted; it's not God's intention for your life. Remember the Sabbath Day? 2) When you feel tired, get away with God. Relax, pray, read, renew. When the leader is tired, temptation has just enjoyed a double espresso.

Times of crisis and defeat can also lead to temptation. There are moments when even leaders have wondered if it's all worth it. When you preach your best sermon and someone criticizes your theology. When the plan you had wasn't endorsed at the board meeting. When the leader you've nurtured disappoints you. When the friend you thought you had stabs you in the back. The leader sometimes feels like quitting. Paying attention to times of crisis is a valuable practice in our battle against sin.

Another valuable practice for preventing a major stumble is the identification of places where temptation most likely occurs. Sometimes temptation really can be avoided by simply "staying off the porch." If you see a woman bathing on the porch, staying in the house will eliminate the temptation. If you have a problem with Internet porn, get rid of the computer. If you watch dirty movies late at night, get rid of the movie channels or satellite dish. Don't stop at the magazine stands in airports if you are drawn to the flesh there. If a certain person seems flirtatious or has wrong intentions, avoid her.

> "Avoid every kind of evil"
> (1 Thessalonians 5:22).

The wise leader will pay attention to all that we have mentioned. He will expect temptation to come, will know the form temptation most often takes in his heart, will be able to identify key times and certain places where it's likely to hit. These are beginning places for dealing with temptations, but as this story of king David shows, there are specific leadership temptations.

When the temptation comes, many leaders are tempted further to justify their actions because of the leadership position they hold. David may have reasoned, "I'm the king. No one will deny me. I've done so much for God. I deserve another wife." Some leaders are tempted to think that because they are serving God they have certain exemptions. Leaders who get wrapped up in privileges that others on their team do not share must be careful; it may allow Satan to get a foot in the door.

Besides justifying sin because of their position, some leaders reason that no one will find out. This is rarely true. Most often sexual sin will be brought to light. If it weren't for Bathsheba's pregnancy, David still would have been found out. The prophet would probably still have come. God always knows. Leaders know that God will forgive them. This is the grace that they lead others to. It is easy to believe that God will forgive us and no one else will ever find out.

Sometimes a leader may try to hide his temptation. This is very common. So often the leader feels as if there is no one he can trust with his innermost struggles. Unfortunately, at most churches this is true. The people they lead have often put them on such a high pedestal they believe their leaders are incapable of giving in to temptation. Sometimes this influences the leader to believe that he can't share his sins for fear of bursting the bubbles of the people. The bigger fear may be that any confession of temptation, struggle, or sin may result in losing his job. This is why a trusted person with just the right mix of mercy and justice is invaluable to the leader. If you don't have a person like this, seek one out.

> "Therefore confess your sins to each other and pray for each other so that you may be healed." (James 5:16).

As I write this chapter, I am reflecting on many leadership friends of mine. One got hooked on Internet chat rooms and finally acted out the fantasy he was typing. The marriage is done, and so is his leadership credibility. I think of another who was crushed by a one-time affair that came back to haunt him years later. His days of influencing people for God are over. Yet another got a girl in the youth group pregnant. The church fired him, and the girls' parents sued him. Many friends have confided that their marriage is in shambles, and they are attracted to someone else. They are standing on the porch watching someone take a shower. Soon they will fall.

It's winter now. Snow is falling gently in the courtyard. A king stares at the white-capped Mount Hermon in the distance

> There is only one time in the Bible where we find it snowing. (See 2 Samuel 23:20.)

and thinks of his friend Uriah. A cold tear streaks his face. He pulls his wrap around his head and returns to the warmth of the palace fires. He sings a now familiar song:

"Wash away all my iniquity and cleanse me from my sin. For I know my transgressions, and my sin is always before me. . . . Cleanse me with hyssop, and I will be clean; wash me, and I will be whiter than snow. . . . Create in me a pure heart, O God, and renew a steadfast spirit within me. . . . Do not cast me from your presence or take your Holy Spirit from me" (Psalm 51:2-11).

This is a prayer for every leader who has ever given in to temptation. This is David's prayer of repentance. This is your prayer, dear leader.

CHAPTER THIRTEEN
Leading the Impossible Victories

"This is what the LORD says: Make this valley full of ditches. For this is what the LORD says: You will see neither wind nor rain, yet this valley will be filled with water, and you and your cattle and your other animals will drink. This is an easy thing in the eyes of the LORD" (2 Kings 3:16-18).

"The next morning, about the time for offering the sacrifice, there it was—water flowing from the direction of Edom! And the land was filled with water" (2 Kings 3:20).

"Hezekiah received the letter from the messengers and read it. Then he went up to the temple of the LORD and spread it out before the LORD. And Hezekiah prayed to the LORD. . ." (2 Kings 19:14).

"Hezekiah turned his face to the wall and prayed to the LORD, 'Remember, O LORD, how I have walked before you faithfully and with wholehearted devotion and have done what is good in your eyes.' And Hezekiah wept bitterly" (2 Kings 20:2-3).

Sometimes leadership is easy. There are personnel decisions in the church that are as elementary as comparing candidates and choosing. The collective "duh" from the congregation is a dead giveaway. Some financial decisions can be made with little more than a comprehension of fourth grade math (of course there are more zeros and fewer pictures, but you get the point). Many times, a spiritual issue can be resolved with some prayer and teaching on a simple passage from Scripture. Not every leadership day is filled with stress-filled decisions of eternal consequence.

> "How is never a problem for God. It is usually a big problem for us. But how is God's specialty. If the Old and New Testament teach us anything, they teach us that nothing is too difficult for God."
>
> Andy Stanley, *Visioneering* (Sisters, OR: Multnomah, 1999), p. 56.

But in those moments where the odds are stacked against you and the task, goal, or opposition seems insurmountable, the leader really earns his paycheck. Our senior pastor says, "Ninety-five percent of the decisions we make could be made by a high school student. It's the other five percent we get paid for." Although they seem to be less frequent, impossible obstacles do arise in the course of leading God's people. Leadership in these times separates the good leaders from the great ones.

Jehoshaphat and Hezekiah, both kings of Judah, were great leaders because of the incredible victories they led their people to. As we stroll through their battlefields and palaces, observe challenges and decisions which led to impossible victories.

> Jehoshaphat was king over Judah in Jerusalem from 874–850 BC.

> "Archeologists have found a number of board games, indicating their wide popularity in ancient Near Eastern cultures. A game board with 14 round playing pieces was found at Ur, dating from the 26th century BC."
> Jill Maynard, *Bible Life and Times* (Pleasantville, NY: Reader's Digest Association, 1997), p. 149.

Jehoshaphat was sitting in his palace one day playing checkers with one of the guards. "King me!" he shouted, reveling in the fact that he really was king. The game was interrupted by a messenger from the northern king of Israel. One of Israel's neighboring countries, Moab had revolted, refusing to pay taxes. The king of Israel wondered if he could count on the support of the southern king to bring them back into subjection. Jehoshaphat agreed to help by joining forces with his Hebrew brothers. The two kings and their armies marched south to Edom.

As they approached Edom's border, they sent a message ahead to Edom's king and asked not only for passage but also to join the battle. It was a really slow day in Edom, so the king called together all his men and these three kings (I'm struggling with the strong temptation to make a Christmas hymn joke) combined their forces that day. Everything was proceeding according to plan. There was no way the army of Moab could defeat these three allies. Victory was sure. It was only a matter of time.

On the seventh day of this massive campaign against Moab, the outlook changed. "Excuse me, King, sir," a commander hesitantly remarked. "I don't know how to tell you this, but there seems to be a problem with our water supply."

"What is it?"

"We're out, Your Highness."

Immediately, the king of Israel despaired, "This is just great. Three armies ready for battle and we're going to die of thirst out here in the desert."

Jehoshaphat, the king of Judah, stepped up to the leadership plate and asked if there was a prophet around. Surely there was a holy man who could give them some insight from God. One of the men suggested they give Elisha a call, and before you know it, the legendary prophet stood before the three leaders. There was definitely some tension since Israel's king had hardly been living a godly life. "Why don't you ask your false prophets to save you," Elisha glared. "If it weren't for King Jehoshaphat here who follows God, I wouldn't give you the time of day, but for his sake I'll inquire of God."

After he called for a harp and meditated before the Lord, Elisha had a word from God for this army with a water shortage.

The first person to ever play a harp was Jubal the son of Lamech. (See Genesis 4:21.)

"Have your men dig this valley full of ditches," God instructed. God promised to supply them with water, and He also promised to bring them victory over the armies of Moab.

Imagine this leadership moment. First, Jehoshaphat had to convince his king allies that they should follow the words of the Lord's prophet. It did seem like a silly and impossible course of action, but soon the other monarchs were on board. Now to communicate with the enlisted men. They were probably already thirsty and cognizant of the fact that the water was gone. To trade in their weapons for shovels and work until sundown making trenches in the desert would deplete the energy they had left and make them even more thirsty. And besides this, how would digging ditches bring them water? Many of these soldiers didn't have a blind allegiance to God. At least two-thirds of this allied force weren't God followers at all.

However, Jehoshaphat led these three armies to trust in God's ability to deliver. He knew what the prophet had said was true. Supplying water for all of these guys with their animals seemed impossible, but it would be an easy thing in the eyes of the Lord. When the king of Judah retired to his tent for the evening, he offered a prayer and slept soundly knowing God would deliver.

The next morning's sunrise brought the results Jehoshaphat had expected. It had not rained. The night had been clear and calm, but every ditch in the valley was filled with fresh water flowing from Edom. The men and animals drank their fill, and God was still at work.

As the Moabite scouts looked out on the valley, the sunrise made the water look red. They surmised that the armies had turned on each other in the night and this was blood flowing instead of water. With this report, the king of Moab ordered his troops to advance to the spoil. When they reached the camp, however, the Moabites found three refreshed armies at full strength. This alliance, led by Jehoshaphat and blessed by God's miraculous intervention, brought about an impossible victory over the forces of Moab.

Hezekiah's story fifteen chapters later is not much different. Instead of one of Judah's subjects revolting, it was God's people who had broken from their oppressors. The Lord had inspired the king of Judah to refuse payment of taxes to the Assyrian king. Of course, this caused the king to muster his troops and march towards Jerusalem prepared for war. Along the way, he overthrew the northern kingdom of Israel and then advanced on Judah's northern cities. Messengers from the pagan king brought the threat of defeat in both verbal and written forms.

During this era in world history, there was no one more powerful than Sennacherib, king of Assyria. He had conquered much of the known world and had developed his armies into an incredible war machine. He had superior military equipment, fighters, and strategies. And he arrogantly boasted of his successes. In Jerusalem his messengers loudly proclaimed the coming terror for the people of Judah. They publicly disgraced king Hezekiah and his God in the hearing of the people sitting on the city wall. Panic set in and news hit the front page of the *Jerusalem Times*: "Impending Doom, Evil King Advances to Capital City."

> "Assyria derived its name apparently from Asshur, the son of Shem, Gen. 10:22, who in later times was worshipped by the Assyrians as their chief god."
> William Smith, *Smith Bible Dictionary* (Nashville: Thomas Nelson, 1962), p. 62.

Hezekiah faced this impossible leadership situation the same way he faced so many of his challenges. He put on sackcloth and headed to the temple. He carried the written decree of Sennacherib into the courtyard and laid it before the Lord with his face to the ground as he prayed. "God, this king is making a mockery of your Name. Sure, he's defeated other kingdoms and their 'gods,' but they were just statues made of stone and wood. You are the real God. Come deliver us and show him who's boss."

It wasn't long before Isaiah came knocking with a message from God. The prophet told the king not to worry, God would take care of everything. He promised Hezekiah that not one arrow would be shot in Jerusalem. During the night, God sent his angel into the Assyrian camp and killed 185,000 men. The next morning, seeing all the dead bodies, Sennacharib had no choice but to retreat. He had lost his entire army. He was powerful, but he had never faced a living God before. Hezekiah had led the people of God to an incredible victory against impossible odds.

As we go to school on the history of God in the lives of His leaders, let's begin with a discussion about the "impossible." A reflection upon the task of Christian leadership may cause some people to conclude the entire idea of leading for God is quite impossible. Leading for God means person after person, task after task, lesson after lesson, decision after decision, and problem after problem in a never-ending carousel of church leadership. These facets of leadership are the norm. These happen week after week, day after day.

This chapter is not about those everyday challenges we all face. It's about the big ones, the ones that grab our attention by virtue of their impossibility. At the risk of sounding incredibly unspiritual, not every ministry decision is one that requires God's miraculous power. This is not to say that the leader doesn't need God's power to lead all the time. But honestly, choosing the font for the bulletin, or the theme for this fall's sermon series, or the type of lighting for the sanctuary is hardly a God-sized challenge. God's spiritual gifting to leaders allows them to make these

> "I believe that spiritually gifted leaders construct, over time, a value system and experience base that wisely informs each subsequent decision they make."
>
> Bill Hybels, *Courageous Leadership* (Grand Rapids: Zondervan, 2002), p. 163.

kinds of decisions without too much worry. You will know the impossible ones by the feeling of nausea that sweeps over you as you realize you have to lead through this challenge. Quitting will come to mind. Retreating, crying, running, complaining, and blaming others will all come to mind in these instances, but you're the leader and you must lead.

What kind of impossible odds are we talking about here? Obviously, no armies are likely to advance against our church parking lot anytime soon. What modern day challenge does the Christian leader face that compares to war? The public moral failure of one of your staff members is an impossible challenge. A theological issue that threatens to split the church is a daunting problem. Not meeting budget and having to make hard spending decisions (such as laying off some staff) will feel like a siege against the soul. Engaging in any kind of building program with a vision will seem impossible. The tragic death or diagnosis of a terminal illness to a prominent leader or member of your church will involve large challenges.

The question is how to lead in these situations. The assumption is that leaders pray all the time about everything, even those things that don't seem to present an enormous challenge. On the other hand, prayer takes on a different tone when we identify challenges which are beyond us. Even Jesus taught that some demons just come right out and others need fasting and prayer. The next few pages are about those pesky demons who just won't go away. This is about facing the leadership challenges that are humanly impossible. When those impossible things come our way, we would be wise to follow the steps to victory we see illustrated in the lives of Jehoshaphat and Hezekiah.

The first step to a great victory is the identification of a challenge that will require miraculous intervention. When the three armies ran out of water, Jehoshaphat didn't try to come up with some grand plan to find a water source. His leadership abilities helped him to immediately identify a challenge beyond his strength. When Hezekiah was presented with a threatening letter from this powerful opponent, he didn't compose a courageous response or try to negotiate. He knew this was serious.

As simple as it seems, the beginning of an impossible victory is to label a challenge "impossible." Great leadership is the ability to identify the real issues. People do a lot of things under duress—

some cry, some are quiet, some deny, some get mad. Leaders pull the team together and let them know that they recognize the challenge as significant. This is not a hysterical voice of despair but a reassuring voice of faith in God and an understanding of the seriousness of the challenge. It is both vulnerable and confident. The presence of the leader in this setting is helpful to the team.

You may recall the calming effect George Bush had on the country as he appeared on national television to speak about the events of September 11, 2001. He really didn't have any answers, he simply identified the enemy and the challenge that lay ahead. Consequently, America's fear subsided.

The leader who can't or won't identify the major challenges for his people will not be able to lead them well. This will leave them feeling that their leader doesn't know or doesn't care. Neither is an acceptable leadership stance.

When the leader has identified the impossibility, he next needs to lead the people to seek God. The first words out of Jehoshaphat's mouth were, "Surely there's a prophet of God around here. Let's hear from the Lord." In the same way, Hezekiah rushed to the temple and humbly sought God through prayer. Great Christian leaders will develop this same kind of prayer reflex in response to the impossible. Church leaders who win impossible victories automatically turn to God quickly and call their people to follow them.

This is leadership, because it testifies to those whom we are leading that we understand the seriousness of the situation. It also communicates that we recognize God's power to save. Great leaders have learned that Elisha's words are true: "This is an easy thing in the eyes of the Lord." Our quick turn to God teaches our people to learn to believe in His strength. They can tell whether our prayer is sincere or not. When you pour your heart out before God in front of your people, you are influencing them more than ever.

By turning to God, the leader is also able to cut through the physical challenge and direct people towards the eternal struggle. Great leaders seek a solution for God's sake. The focus is spiritual and the goal is to bring glory to God. While the men in Hezekiah's court were concerned for their lives and the security of their city, Hezekiah was on the floor asking God to glorify His name. The people saw the damage the invaders could do to them personally, but Hezekiah identified the affront this wicked king was to God's honor.

While the men in Hezekiah's court were concerned for their lives and the security of their city, Hezekiah was on the floor asking God to glorify His name.

In extremely tense times, the Christian leader is quick to identify the spiritual implications of the challenge. This helps take the focus off of the imminent danger and places it in the spiritual realm where it belongs. In a strange kind of way, the idea that these impossible challenges are being fought in heavenly places brings surprising calm in the most difficult times. The two challenges seemed to be no water and an advancing army, but these two kings understood that God had access to water and angelic warriors to fight.

The leader is able to move forward with confidence that God will deliver. Hezekiah and Jehoshaphat had extreme confidence in God. This gave those who followed confidence in their leadership. When water filled the valley the next morning, Jehoshaphat wasn't surprised. When the Assyrian king retreated, Hezekiah only smiled. They had faith that God would come through.

Are impossible victories that easy? No, that's why they are called impossible. Even as I write, I realize there is no way I can express through the written word how it feels to be overwhelmed in these leadership moments. Listing four steps to impossible victories seems a bit trite. It's more complicated than that. But I do know that God continues to do the impossible in His church today. Seasoned leaders will lead into the impossible by identifying the situation, praying for God's help, seeking His glory, and moving forward with confidence.

Follow God's Thread

This chapter highlights two instances where the threads were pretty obvious. God delivered in both circumstances, bringing water to a dry valley and causing an army to flee in terror.

CHAPTER FOURTEEN

Legacy

"He walked in all the ways of Jeroboam son of Nebat and in his sin, which he caused Israel to commit, so that they provoked the LORD, the God of Israel, to anger by their worthless idols" (1 Kings 16:26).

"He did what was right in the eyes of the LORD, just as his father David had done. He removed the high places, smashed the sacred stones and cut down the Asherah poles. He broke into pieces the bronze snake Moses had made, for up to that time the Israelites had been burning incense to it" (2 Kings 18:3-4).

Ready for a word association game? I say, "George Washington" and you say "father of our country." I say, "Martin Luther King" and you say, "I have a dream. . . ." Bill Gates—Microsoft computers. Henry Ford—automobiles. Wright brothers—first in flight. Einstein—e=mc². James Brown—the godfather of soul. Elvis—the king. Muhammad Ali—the greatest. Mother Theresa—caring for lepers in India.

> "All individual leaders, no matter how charismatic or visionary, eventually die; and all visionary products and services—all 'great ideas'—eventually become obsolete."
>
> James Collins and Jerry Porras, *Built to Last* (New York: Harper Collins, 1997), p. 31.

Isn't it funny that a name carries so much with it? Given the names listed above most would have come up with the same or similar responses. Each name represents an ideal or accomplishment that this person embodied in his or her lifetime. Most influenced a culture. Many began a revolution. Others changed life as we know it. All have directly or indirectly touched millions of lives. This small sampling of the human race has left something behind. Something they did or stood for will outlive them and influence others for generations to come. They have a legacy.

Legacy is not something most people think about when they are young. Many times the ambition and energy of the young church leader focuses on what is next. But every leader will come to a time when he wonders in a series of internal conversations whether or not he will leave something behind. Most leaders want to influence those around them in the here and now. But great leaders desire to lead in such a way that they continue to impact people long after they have gone. They want a legacy.

A casual reading of the history of Israel's kings (which is where this book began) will reveal two dominant legacies. All the kings of both Israel and Judah had accomplishments. Most of them won wars. Some of them had some wealth. Some of them brought great leadership to their country. Others promoted the gods and practices of the nations around them. A few brought religious reform and pointed the people back to God. Two left a lasting impression upon the history of nearly every one of God's Old Testament leaders.

When a king was evil there was a legacy to which he was compared. There was a measurement that summed up all of his life after the accomplishments were listed. As each history recorded the number of years he reigned and how and where he died, there was a phrase added that described an ungodly king. He was said to have walked in the ways of Jeroboam the son of Nebat who caused Israel to sin by getting the people to worship worthless idols. Leading Israel to idolatry was the legacy of Jeroboam's life.

On the other end of the spectrum were those leaders for the kingdom of Judah who were godly. Each of their stories were told in the same fashion as the others. Their accomplishments and reforms were mentioned along with their ages at death and the years they were king. Then the phrase of honor would be attached to their names. Of these it was said, "He did what was right in the eyes of the Lord just as his father David had done." This was David's legacy, and they made it theirs.

> Eight of the twenty kings of Judah were said to have followed God to some degree, but of the nineteen kings of Israel none were righteous.

Before we examine how each of these kings established a legacy, let's ask if it is important for a leader to have one. Consider this: someday you will not be in charge. Sooner or later, someone else will take your place of leadership. No matter how gifted you are, another will assume your position. We know these statements to be true because, barring the Lord's return, we know that all of us will die. Here's a strange leadership question to ponder: after you're dead, how will you lead?

You've probably never thought of it (unless you're a dreamer or nearing the end of a long leadership journey), but all you'll have left at the end of your life is a legacy. You'll be remembered by what those you leave behind learned from you. You will be associated with the things you stood for. More of who you are may be revealed after you're gone than while you're here. Your leadership success will be measured in whether or not your life still matters long after you're dead. And, amazingly, you may be able to lead people by what you're remembered by, associated with, and stood for in your lifetime. Such was the case with David and Jeroboam.

God gave the kingdom of Israel to Jeroboam on a silver platter. One day, as he was doing his job as Solomon's director of labor, a prophet named Ahijah came to him. He may have been busy supervising a new park, an aqueduct, or another palace for another one of Solomon's queens. It was one of those days when it just didn't pay to get out of bed, and to top it all off, he hears there's a prophet on the work site—in a construction zone with no hard hat.

> Ahijah is interchangeable with the name Ahiah and means "the friend of God."

Jeroboam went to gently rebuke Ahijah, but before he could get a word out, the man of God grabbed him and ripped his new flannel off his back. He proceeded to tear the garment into twelve pieces. Jeroboam looked at the prophet in disbelief. The prophet only responded by telling him to pick ten pieces of the garment. This was an illustration that God was ripping ten tribes away from Solomon and giving them to Jeroboam. Pay attention to this. Jeroboam was handpicked by God.

> The apostle Paul also had a piece of his clothing used in a prophecy about him. The prophet Agabus took the apostle's belt and symbolized Paul's imprisonment by binding his own hands."

Jeroboam was promised a kingdom like that of David's. The Lord promised that if Jeroboam obeyed and followed His lead, he would have descendants on his throne like that of David. God was keeping David's line on the throne of Judah, but he was breaking up Solomon's kingdom because he had introduced so much idolatry into the country. God and Jeroboam had an agreement.

Of course, things got a little rocky once Solomon heard about this arrangement. The king turned on his once-trusted official and tried to kill him. Jeroboam had to flee to Egypt to save his life. Not long after that, Solomon passed on and his son, Rehoboam, made his fateful decision. And who was there to capture the hearts of the disgruntled Israelites? Jeroboam. In a matter of time he became king over this newly formed part of God's people and reigned in Shechem. Unfortunately, he did not trust God to deliver what He had promised him.

Jeroboam reasoned that if these Israelites had to continue going to Jerusalem for church, they would eventually become loyal to Rehoboam again and would kill him as a rebel. To prevent this from happening, he set up two golden calves

> Israel had history with a golden calf. It was this same type of idol that Aaron had fashioned in the wilderness while Moses was on the mountain. (See Exodus 32:4.)

(probably an adaptation of the idolatry he had learned from his time spent in Egypt) and set them in places of worship in the cities of Bethel and Dan.

The northern kingdom of Israel never again worshiped the true God. The people of the break-off nation and their kings continued in idol worship until they were conquered and destroyed. Not one king considered following God. Even though God had promised Jeroboam a continuous line on the throne under God's leadership, Jeroboam instead led the people away from Him. He influenced the entire history of a nation for bad. He left a legacy of idolatry.

David's story is better known. Most know him well, but let's review a godly legacy in the making. As a young shepherd boy his heart warmed to God's emotion through song. As a young man, God used his passion for Him to conquer the Philistine champion. As the anointed king of Israel, he fled from his jealous predecessor, but he maintained his integrity. When he established

Jerusalem as the town of David, he led the worship procession. He sinned big, but he repented even bigger. His heart beat with God. He had a passion for God. He truly loved God. He obeyed God.

Those who came after David had a positive example. Many were great warriors in God's name. Some were great worshipers who led people to the throne of God with their promotion of God's ways. A few of these kings had hearts that, like David's, were in touch with God's emotions. And when these leaders came along, they were compared to David. He left a legacy of following after God.

What kind of legacy can today's Christian leader hope to leave behind? Will we influence a generation? Will our leadership lives stir a movement like Martin Luther's reformation? Could we write theology to change the thinking of Christian intelligentsia? We may not do something so grand . . . and then again, it is perhaps the calling God has given us.

It is certain, however, that we will inevitably leave small legacies everywhere we go. If a student from your church is called to preach, whose style do you think he will emulate? Where will the men of your congregation learn to love their wives and lead their families? Who will teach people about grace? How will future church leaders have the ability to balance corporate wisdom with spiritual passion? These are the legacies we develop every day as we lead for God.

This means we as leaders stand at a legacy crossroads. One path leads to leaving a legacy of negative impact. The other path (which I'm sure is narrower and more of an uphill climb) will take us to the positive legacy we all desire.

> "Enter through the narrow gate. For wide is the gate and broad is the road that leads to destruction and many enter through it. But small is the gate and narrow the road that leads to life and only a few find it" (Matthew 7:13).

Jeroboam does have some value to us as leaders. He serves as a bad example. "How not to" is the name of his leadership book. Jeroboam began his negative legacy by ignoring God. If you'll examine the Scripture, you'll see that when Solomon sought to take Jeroboam's life, the king-to-be didn't consult God. God had just promised him that he would be the king of ten tribes. When God tells you that you're king, there is no need to run to Egypt as Jeroboam did.

What would have happened if Jeroboam had stayed away from Egyptian influence and sought God on what to do with Solomon? We don't know for sure, God may have sent a message to Solomon telling him to back off. All we know is God had a plan and Jeroboam didn't seem to consult Him in order to follow it.

> ## Follow God's Thread
>
> We observe through the life of Jeroboam a thread of God and His faithfulness in our obedience. God's promises are true, but our obedience is required. God had promised Jeroboam greatness, but in the end his disobedience removed him from the leadership role God had bestowed.

If you ignore God in your leadership, you will leave a negative legacy. Jeroboam was successful by worldly standards and you may achieve praise from men. But your spiritual legacy will be a bad one. When you drift from God's plan, you will soon lead by the world's standards and, when you're gone, someone will discover that though you were a religious leader by title, you weren't by heart. History doesn't lie. Time has a way of revealing truth. Lead without God, and your long term impact will be despised.

Once he began ignoring God, there was only one logical progression. He started paying attention to himself. This is where Jeroboam really went wrong. He began to care more about his title and position than he did anything else. He cared more about losing the kingdom than he did sending the people to the right place (the temple in Jerusalem) to worship the Living God. His ambition got in the way, and before long he wasn't leading people, he was using them to retain the power he loved. He deceived them into worshiping God in the form of a calf for the sole purpose of keeping his crown. This was very selfish indeed.

A leader who cares more about retaining the power and prestige of a title or a position of leadership will eventually manipulate those he leads to keep it. This is not leadership, it is self-worship. This egocentric attitude turns followers into pawns. They are only there to be played for the benefit of the leader. Of course, there is no place for this kind of legacy in any church or Christian organization. The deceit, power, and pride of such leaders has destroyed the spiritual vitality in all too many churches.

David left a positive legacy because he led in a totally different way. Look closely at his life, and you will see a king who above all seeks God. People followed him because they were convinced he had a connection with the Almighty, and he did. David spent time with God and those who followed him knew it. Why was he able to rally so many wild men to his side? Because he called them to something bigger than himself. He called them to fight, worship, give, and live for God. It was this motivation to serve God that he always promoted and the people remembered it when he was dead.

Today's leader must constantly ask, "What am I calling my people to?" Are you calling them to something that God desires? Are you pointing them in the direction of His dreams? Is God and His kingdom the driving force? If the answer to these questions is "no," then you are probably calling people to your goals and dreams and visions. The encouragement is to get away with God and let Him put a cause on your heart that will leave a positive legacy.

David also left a positive legacy because he regularly invested in his people. David cared for those around him. He thought about the men's wives and children when they were on the run from enemies. When victory came, he rewarded those who helped. His deep love for Jonathan probably indicates the kind of passion he had for many of those who worked for him. He cared about the people around him.

One way to leave something positive behind is to leave it deep in the heart of someone who lives after you die. This a simple but profound truth. Leaders who spend quality time with a selected few have a legacy. Your church will forget your charisma. Your church will move on from your great preaching. The way you ran a meeting will not be remembered. But sharing your spiritual journey intimately with a selected few will continue your influence long after you're gone.

Dedicating extra time to staff members or lay people with the highest growth potential will be wise investments for the future. Jesus did this with His inner circle of Peter, James, and John. When He left the earth, they carried on his ministry because of His intense training in their lives. In the same way, those who are able to see your heart for God will carry on that passion when you're gone. Those who knew David knew he loved God, and they reminded everyone of it until it became part of Jewish culture. To live for God was to be like David. Several kings were honored with a comparison to David. In this way, his legacy also became theirs.

As a leader, you are likely to leave a legacy. Someone is going to catch your attitudes, words, faith, and walk. This legacy may be big or it may be small, but when all is said and done, you will have one.

Two leaders. One idolatrous. One obedient. Both remembered.

What will be remembered about you?

One Leadership Lesson

We began on a simple quest. Our agenda was to observe the lives of the leaders God used as kings for His people and in the process learn about leadership. Throughout this journey we have pointed out several leadership principles and observed leadership at its best and worst. Hopefully, we have grown in our leadership, but is there one thing we can take from all these stories? What counsel will properly summarize the reigns of these leaders and God's work in their lives? What can we take from these kings and their stories? The answer is similar to the statement mentioned in the introduction.

Woven throughout the lives of all leaders in all places in all times, is the consistent thread of God's eternal will and purpose. Throughout this book we have noted several threads of God's will woven into every story. These have been observations of His work in the midst of the lives of His leaders. In this historical period of God's people we have seen His movement and direction through prophets, priests, and kings that became the tapestry for salvation.

This means that ministers, pastors, paid and volunteer leaders, elders and deacons, parachurch directors, and Christian college presidents can all rest assured that God is at work in their leadership. As leaders we must never forget this truth. It overcomes our weaknesses and mistakes. It energizes us and drives our passion. It directs our vision and moves us heavenward. God's kingdom will prevail, and as unbelievable as it may seem at times, He will use *us* to accomplish His purpose. There are several implications to this idea of God weaving an eternal tapestry that represents His movement among His people.

136

First, God is constantly weaving. This means that on the tapestry of humankind, God is not always visible but He is still working. There were many times in the lives of these kings that we may have wondered where God was, but sure enough in His timing and His way, His presence and working was made evident. It may have been just a thread, but it was an integral part of the whole. Sometimes His thread was bright and obvious and dominated all surrounding colors. At other times, the thread was more subtle and barely even noticeable. However, as leaders we can never forget that the thread is there, and God is weaving.

No matter your leadership situation, the thread of God's will is there. If your life is twisted with the cords of leadership failure, public sin, or continued resistance, an unraveling will reveal God's grace intertwined with it all. If you are experiencing the victories of success, wisdom, and endurance, you will do well to identify these as God's colors woven brilliantly into your setting. God never leaves the cloth of humanity and is therefore never absent from the lives of those who lead His people.

Not only is God constantly weaving, but He is weaving with His people. As leaders, we are the threads that God is using. We can rest assured that God is working in every leader for His purpose. Obviously, not every king got as much press as others. Some of these ancient leaders were famous because they had several chapters devoted to them. For others, only a few verses summarized their reigns. But all of them were valuable in the scheme of God's kingdom plan. He moved in each leader's life to create the perfect setting for a Savior. Each of these leaders contributed in some way, great or small, righteous or wicked to the national history of Judah and/or Israel. This is significant because out of this history was born the Son of God, the Messiah.

No matter who you are, if leadership is your gift, God has designed you to be a part of the leadership of His kingdom. You may not get the recognition like many well-known theologians. Your ministry ideas may never be touted as cutting edge. You might never preach to millions or write books that are bestsellers. But you are a thread that God is sewing into the fabric of His kingdom. This kingdom doesn't point to the salvation of a promised Messiah, but to the return of a conquering King. If you are faithful and allow God to lead you as you lead others, your life will ultimately be a part of a greater whole that is eternal in its significance.

The leader will also realize one final truth about this cosmic tapestry of God's making. God is weaving today. Since God is using us as the thread, He must be working in our individual settings each and every day. Until the angelic trumpet sounds, signifying the return of our Lord, every day is a day in which God is working. He has not stopped laying visions on the hearts of His leaders or moving miraculously in their lives or honoring righteous prayers. He is at work today and He is at work where you are. Some of us have lamented, "I want to be part of a work that God is doing." What we sometimes forget is that God is at work everywhere, every day. We are a part of God's work! Again, it may not always be that obvious, but He is there nonetheless.

Throughout this book we have made notations in the margins of significant facts about certain kings. We have noted the movements, warnings, and guidance of various prophets. We have also witnessed the influence of priests in the stories of these kings. These three offices were used by God in the Old Testament to accomplish His will in the lives of His people. In those rare times when prophet, priest, and king were all following Him, God's people flourished by God's hand. Many times, however, one or more of these offices were occupied by ungodly men which led the people into disobedience and brought punishment from God.

These offices were also a foreshadowing of something to come. The prophets, priests, and kings of the Old Testament were all pointing to a day when the Messiah would come and fill all three roles. At just the right time, God pulled out His eternal loom and began to weave the centerpiece of His human tapestry. In this act, He became flesh and dwelled among men and so reclaimed His rightful place as Prophet, Priest, and King. Finally, God was on the throne again where He belonged.

This is the part of the story where we could give counsel to the kings. Many of the kings who sat on the thrones of Israel and Judah only understood their title. Because they were king, they had power to lead. This is why they often focused on building their earthly kingdom. Most of them had no idea that God was willing to help them, guide them, protect them, and empower them to accomplish heavenly things. They missed the point of godly leadership.

The point of godly leadership is to discover how He wants to use us to advance the cause of His salvation work. We have experienced God in the flesh. He wants to love us, guide us, protect us, and empower us to lead others to His eternal purpose. He has called us to lead people in a direction that has "forever" implications. This is not an earthly kingdom, it is a kingdom not of this world.

The most important leadership lesson is one that the kings could never teach us. Ultimately, great leadership will come from sitting in the counsel not of the kings, but of the King.